SRI GURU NANAK DEV JI WAS THE FIRST GURU AND FOUNDER OF SIKHISM

CHERISHED EVENTS OF THE LIFE OF PEHLI PATSHAHI, SRI GURU NANAK DEV JI

By

Bhai Sahib Dr. Vir Singh

Translated By
Ujagar Singh Bawa
M.A. (Punjab), A.M. (Pennsylvania), Ph.D. (Cornell)
Professor of Economics
Bloomsburg University of Pennsylvania

The Washington Sikh Center
The Sikh Youth Forum
P.O. Box 7061
Gaithersburg, MD 20898

Produced entirely in the United States of America.

Library of Congress Catalog Number: 88-51038
Main entry under title: CHERISHED EVENTS, Sri Guru Nanak Dev Ji

Translation of Punjabi version of Balam Sakhian, Pehli Patshahi.
Also sections from Sri Guru Granth Sahib depicting Sikh way of life.

Singh, Vir and Bawa, Ujagar Singh

ISBN: 0-942245
ISBN: 0-942245-04-0 (Paperback)

Published in April, 1989 by
The Washington Sikh Center
The Sikh Youth Forum
P.O. Box 7061
Gaithersburg, MD 20798

Donation: $5.00

ACKNOWLEDGEMENTS

I owe a debt of gratitude to Bhai Vir Singh Sahitya Sadan, New Delhi for kindly giving their permission to bring out an English version of the original title, Balam Sakhian, Pehli Patshahi for the benefit of English-knowing readers.

Ujagar Singh Bawa

The financing of this book by modest but generous, kind, and anonymous donors, is gratefully acknowledged.

All monies raised through the sale of this book and other books published by The Washington Sikh Center and The Sikh Youth Forum have been assigned for use for Sikh children programs.

Ujagar Singh Bawa

Dedicated to the memory
of
Bhai Sahib Sant Sujan Singh Ji
Baganwale

CONTENTS

PREFACE

Time and again, I have confessed that it is exceeding difficult to portray the innermost true sentiments of the original author when his work is translated into any other language. I concede that where we do lose a part of sensitivity and discriminatory tasteful fastidiousness intentioned by Bhai Sahib Dr. Vir Singh in his writings, there is a modest gain, though, (in translation) to expose his great works to a wider audience, particularly, the western readership and those children and adults who are not equipped with the facility of Punjabi language. This translation is an humble effort in this direction.

Besides, the intent of this text is to recount the deeds of the First Guru (master), Sri Guru Nanak Dev Ji to show him to be the most remarkable godsent, divine and benevolent soul, and to project his actions for transmitting his moral, religious, and ethical teachings.

There are 65 episodes in this book beginning from his childhood in Sri Nanakana Sahib (Talwandi).

I am thankful to my son, Devinder and his wife, Kanwalpreet for doing an indepth reading/editing of the original manuscript. I sincerely appreciate the assistance of Fern Gallagher of the Word Processing Center, Bloomsburg University of Pennsylvania in typing and processing the manuscript. I also acknowledge the facilities made available by the Bloomsburg University in the production of this book.

I, alone, am responsible for all errors or omissions.

April 2, 1989

Ujagar Singh Bawa
Washington, D.C.

CHILDHOOD EVENTS OF SRI GURU NANAK DEV JI

1. THE HOUSEHOLD OF BELOVED GURU

Our beloved Guru's name is Sri Guru Nanak Dev Ji. He came to this world a little over 500 years ago. At that time, Bailol Lodhi used to rule the country. The year was 1526 Bikrimi. The descending of the Guru from the Lord's land is called manifestation or emanation. He was sent by the Lord so that he could engage the people in noble acts, teach them to love each other and to counsel them to cultivate affinity for the good Lord.

The name of the village where he was born was called 'Rai Bhoi Di Talwandi'. (The original name of this village was Rai Pur, then changed to Rai Bhoi Di Talwandi, and is presently called Nanakana Sahib. It is located in the Sharak Pur Tehsil in the district of Sheikhupura, Pakistan.) This place is about 25 miles west of Lahore.

Guru's mother was BeBe Tripata Ji and the father, Mehta Kalu Ram Ji, but people called him 'Kalu Ji'. He was Khatri by caste but was called 'Bedi'.

What did Kalu Ji do? There were several other villages adjacent to the village where he used to live. The collection of all these villages was called a 'Tapa', something similar to a group of hamlets. This geographical conglomeration had a 'Rai' who was considered a "junior" ruler. His name was 'Rai Bular'. He had appointed Mehta Kalu as his agent and accountant who was responsible to keep accounts of his land, and other transactions, and who would also consummate and coordinate his financial activities so that the Rai didn't have to be personally involved in all these chores.

Mehta Kalu, while he was engaged in several other deals, he was also maintaining the land records as well. That was why, he was also called a 'Patwari', a chief revenue official, also the 'head' of all other revenue officials.

A daughter, named Nanaki, was born to Mehta Kalu in 1521, and she was, out of affection, called Bibi Nanaki. This girl was very affectionate and loving. She was well disposed and conscientious even at a tender age. She used to lend a hand to her mother in several minor household chores, and listen to her discourses about the Almighty. She would tell and listen to stories; delve in puzzles but would get great pleasure from listening to the praises of the Lord and accounts of saintly persons.

At the time, when Bibi would join her playmates for different games, she would also organize and participate in choruses: some of the choruses were about a brother for whom she always longed to be blessed by Waheguru. She would sing couplets such as:

> "Come, O'my brother, your sister is calling you,
> Come, O'handsome brother, your sister is willing to sacrifice herself for you."

2. EMANATION OF GURU JI

Our beloved Guru was born in Mehta Kalu's home when Bibi Nanaki was a little over five years old. When the Guru came down as a little infant, in this house, the entire surrounding was engulfed with an enormous brightness. At the time of his birth, Mehta Kalu sent for his priest (Brahmin), Hardayal. Kalu was a Vedi by caste and Hardayal was the priest of Vedis. What is a priest? Someone from the Brahmanic class who is invited to the people's homes from time to time, but particularly, on the occasions of births, deaths and weddings, and who performs all the appropriate ceremonies. He is bestowed with gifts, charities and donations. He is a learned person, who also engages in imparting teaching and instruction.

Hardayal looked at the horoscope, calculated the nativity and said, "This child will be a great, great man". Then Mehta Kalu asked him, "Will he be a wealthy person?" The family priest explained, "He will be the God's beloved. People will have great faith in him; will accept him as a great prophet; he will direct the masses towards good deeds. He will teach the love for the Lord. Folks! he is God-sent, he is a prophet. Be careful! Do not treat him like any other child."

This child, indeed, would not cry like other children. The mother would nurse him at regular intervals. Unlike ordinary children, he would not cry even when he was hungry. He would keep lying down quietly. He would, sometime look up, here and there; and would sleep at other times. When asleep or otherwise, his face glowed with an unusual brightness and his tiny lips seemed to be adding a smile to his face. This infant would stay in his crib quietly while his mother would go out of the house. Sometimes, his sister would come and fondle him, he would look back towards her, and appeared pleased.

3. CHILDHOOD FROLICS

Growing like this, the God-blessed child became three years old. He was, then, able to talk and play as well. His games were, however, different and unusual. His sister would tell him short stories, and engage him in conversation, during which time, he would say, "Yes, it is there, it is there." Sometimes, he would say, "Look! Look at that? What is there? He is; Yes, He is there." He will, then, raise his arms and say, "Yes, it is Him; it is, indeed, Him." He would utter such tender impressions of coquettishness during the games and story tellings which his folks did not, really, appreciate or understand.

This child was now able to walk around. He would, sometimes, sit down in the middle of the courtyard, squat cross legged and close his eyes. After a little while, he would open his eyes and say, "Yes Sir!" He would, then, join other children in their games of amusement. Whenever, a child would visit him, he would offer him food and butter. Whatever toys his mother would bring for him or the dolls and their clothes that his sister would give to him (out of endearment), this unusual child would give them away. He would not cling to his toys, like other children, and would not claim them as only his own. If the sister would present him with a pair of puppets and ask him to join her to play with them, he would lay them on the ground and say, "Speak, please speak." When they didn't, he would complain to his sister, "Why don't they talk?"

4. CHARITABLE NATURE IN CHILDHOOD

Like this, this handsome child reached 5/6 years of age. He now went out of the house, sometimes. He spoke very well. When he went out, he would be stopped by several men and women who would ask him all kinds of questions. Everyone was simply surprised on his answers, which were completely unchildlike and seemed to be coming from a grown up person. People would remark, "Look at his tender age, and look at his answers full of wisdom." Sometimes, the people were not able to understand his answers. While expressing himself, he would, while saying "Him, Him", run away. People did not appreciate what he was referring to when he said, "Him, Him," or "He is, He is". As he continued to grow, he would speak tacitly, which when understood, would mean talking about God. People became inquisitive to listen to such discourses. When he would come out to sit under trees and shrubs, people would gather around him, ask questions, and would be elated, and somewhat even surprised to listen to his answers. It is mentioned in the classical Janam Sakhi (Story of Birth) that, "As he grew, he started talking about the unapproachable, the peerless, and the inaccessible."

The child by now had developed another trait. When he went out, he would give away anything he had in his hand whenever asked for it. One day, he was carrying a small drinking pot. He ran into an ascetic who said, "O' child! I have no utensil to drink water from. Give me this drinking pot." The Child Guru gave it away immediately. Like this, he gave away several of his household items to the needy. His mother had intense love for him; and she fondled and caressed him excessively, but was concerned about him when she observed this kind of behavior. She would, then, try to reconcile herself by saying, "After all, he is not indulging in any base acts. By giving charities, he is doing virtuous deeds." The father, Kalu, also loved him dearly but got worried about him watching his behavior. He kept wondering if his son was not going crazy. He would, then, approach the family priest and ask him, "You said, that he would be a great man; he is, on the contrary, squandering away all my property." The priest would assuringly tell Kalu Ji, "Dear host! You should not be disheartened or sad. God-sent messengers who come here to comfort the masses, are large hearted and generous by nature. He is the biggest of the benefactors. Do not waiver, and have faith."

Well, what is a 'host'? The Brahmins are called priests and the priests call those persons from whom they receive charities and donations, hosts. Who do we call large hearted or a benefactor? A person who is compassionate and likes to give away things to the needy is considered a large-hearted person, and anyone who actually practices this noble ideal, can be called a benefactor.

5. TEACHER/HINDU PRIEST/SCHOOL MASTER/ASTROLOGER

The father of this promising and beautiful child, Mehta Kalu, told the family priest again on another day, that his son was lavishly wasting and squandering away his assets and asked him as to what should he do? "He is the only son whom I got after yearning, longing and long prayers, I do not feel like spanking him." The priest replied, "O' Host! Send him to school. He should go regularly to the teacher/priest/astrologer. He will learn about preparation of accounts and will be able to conduct his business when he grows older. He will be kept busy with the teacher all day long. But beware, lest you slap him. Don't forget, he is God's beloved."

Mehta Kalu took his son to priest-teacher, named, Gopal. Who was a priest-teacher-astrologer? He was a man who used to run one-room schools at home in the boros. He would teach all his pupils the accounts, totalling, the preparation of the ledgers, and auditing. He would also instruct in writing business letters locally and to out-of-town businessmen. He would teach them the *Mahajani* script (Landa), and coach them with arithmetic tables. Just as we send our children to schools these days to learn to read, write and do arithmetic, people used to send their kids to just one such teacher in the old days.

Mehta took his son to Gopal, a teacher-priest, and said, "Well, please teach my son, too. Teach him all accounts and whatever else you happen to know." Kalu, at the same time, presented the teacher with a tray of sweetmeats and few rupees. The teacher distributed the sweets to all his students and made his newly admitted pupil sit with affection next to himself. He gave Nanak a wooden slate, and wrote on it "*Onam Sidhan*", (Bow before the saints with whose blessing, may you become educated and learned). The children didn't understand this difficult expression on their slates but it was like a blessing from a teacher at the time they were admitted. But this uncommon and charming child, Nanak, read those difficult words with great ease as if he knew them already. Then the teacher put numbers one through ten on his slate. The child was able to write them as well without any difficulty. One day, the teacher told him to write compound words by putting together letters so that after learning word making, he would be able to construct sentences and be able to write business letters anyway his thoughts would direct.

One day, the teacher observing that the child had written a letter asked him, "Child! What have you written?" He replied that he had written the letter 'S' (Sassa), if he added an E sound to it, it became 'Soi'. The teacher inquired surprisingly, "What is 'Soi'?" The elegantly graceful child said, "Ess for Soi". "'Soi' respected teacher! The one who has created us, he is our master-Sire who has forged the entire universe." (Sassa for Sahib—Sire; and Sassa for Srishti—universe).

The priest-teacher hearing this, was flabbergasted. He remained mum for quite a while, and then asked, "Anything else?"

Child: "Dear teacher! Then Ess for Service (Sewa), and anyone who does service for the Sire will be (Ess for) successful."

The teacher in utter surprise, went and sat on his mat, and the child, on the other side, keeping his slate in front of him, sat there quietly with his eyes closed.

This child who should be called a God-sent child, kept going to school for a few more days. One day, the teacher called him and asked, "Son! I taught you the expressions matching each letter. Did you write them?" The child presented his wooden slate before the teacher, and it had a really long expression for the letter 'Ess', that meant the following:

> 'Ess stands for Soi, the Creator, who has created the entire universe, and He is the only Sire-Master for everyone. Those who do service for the Master, their coming to the world is worthwhile and successful.'
>
> [This is a long expression in Sri Guru Granth Sahib written in Raag Asa]

When the teacher read the entire expression, which was quite long, his surprise knew no bounds. Sometimes, he would look towards the child's head and sometimes towards his feet. Then, his head bent down in obeisance, he said to himself, "This little kid knows so much about God at this tender age that even the learned Pandits, in their prime, do not know. May he not be a God-sent prophet?"

6. SERMON TO THE TEACHER

The ever charming child kept going to the priest-teacher; and kept getting some education, too. But after a few days, he would not pay any attention to classroom instruction, and would either keep sitting quietly with eyes closed, or would keep staring on one side. The teacher asked him, "Why don't you be attentive in the class, Son? You can compose well whatever comes to your mind, but it would be better if you could learn some accounts as well."

Then the bewitching and lovable child's eyes became merciful, looked at the teacher sitting on the mat with compassion and said, "Sir! Do not worry about the accounts, and do not teach arithmetic; these can become strangleholds like nooses. You write the name, Ess for Sire, write Ess for sweet praises for Him, who is limitless and eternal."

The teacher, hearing all this, was again astonished. He kept thinking, "this child is already fully knowledgeable. He talks better than even the Pundits. He is even sermonizing as if he has been directed by the Lord." The priest/teacher wanted to ask him some questions to see what kind of answers he would come up with. He asked him, "How would you write His name and His praises?" The god-sent child then said effortlessly, "Dear Sir! Attachment and infatuation with worldly people and things should be burnt out. Use the ashes to make the ink the same way ink is manufactured from popcorn, assume your 'wisdom' with which you impart learning as a paper; then develop a deep fondness for the Lord; this then becomes a writing. Well, dear teacher! A pen. Assume your mind like a small child learning to write, just like me, whom you are teaching to write. Accept someone as your teacher in your heart, a teacher who should steer your way towards the Lord. Ask him and write whatever he says. He will tell you to write His name, and also His praises."

The priest/teacher was further startled but pretending to be unimpressed said with a firm voice, "O' Nanak! If I were to learn this type of accounting, what would happen then? If you can learn my accounting system, you can become a cashier, a treasurer or even an accounts specialist. What will I become by following your above advice?" Then the child looked towards the teacher with compassion again and said, "O' teacher! If you can adopt the accounting system I have described, it will become handy and serve you extremely well when an account of all your actions and deeds will be demanded in the next world. You will be questioned, have you come back after being (Ess for) successful in the mission you had been sent for."

[This thought is expressed by Sri Raag in Sri Guru Granth Sahib]

The teacher kept asking more questions and kept wondering at how eloquently and successfully had this little kid used the letter Ess. He, then, bowed before him and said, "You are not a child; you are a Guru-teacher; you have put my thoughts in the right direction; may Lord bless you. You do whatever you feel like; who am I to teach you." Then, this child returned home. He would keep sitting there, and would not engage himself in any activity. If he would sleep, he would continue doing so for quite a while; and if he would go out and sit outside the village, he would have constant discourses with saints and ascetics about the praises of the Lord.

7. PUNDIT BRIJ NATH

Later, on another day, Mehta Kalu met with family priest and asked, "O' Priest! Would you please look into his horoscope and make some calculations? He is lying around and moping like insane persons, he does not go to his school, nor does he take any interest in his books, he does not read or write, and doesn't do anything. He keeps chattering with ascetics and saints about 'enlightenment'. I am extremely anxious. You are a wise and worldly man; please tell what should I do?"

Hardayal, then told him, "If he is talking about 'enlightenment' at this young age, he may be a great saint or even a prophet. His mind and concentration is towards lofty topics. You should take him to Pundit Brij Nath who can teach him Sanskrit language. (Sanskrit is a classical language of India that was considered scholarly.) Getting instruction from Brij Nath, your son would become a great scholar and a learned man. Incidentally, a child can grow better and become mature and wise if his energies are directed towards his interests and inclinations."

Agreeing to Hardayal's proposal, father Kalu took his son (Nanak) to Brij Nath. He was already inquisitive to see the child who was being talked about all over the town. He wished this child could come to him so that he could know what the matter, really, was. He, therefore, offered him a seat with respect, and wrote a few words in Dev Nagri script in which was written the difficult language, Sanskrit. But, this Godly child wrote those words, too, in no time. He was able to read anything that the Pundit was writing. Pundit was amazed as to where this child got all this sagacity and understanding.

Another day, seeing some piece of paper in his son's hands, Kalu asked him, "What is this?" He replied, "It is Septet Book" (a book containing poetic verses of seven lines each). The father was simply surprised as to how this little child could learn so much in such a short time. He brought his son back to Pundit Brij Nath and narrated him the entire episode. Pundit said, "Son! Just read it." The child then, not only read that book, but also explained the meanings of the verses. The Pundit was stunned and bewildered, and fell at Nanak's feet and said, "Kindly protect this slave. You are the same (Lord) in whose praises this *Septet Book* was written."

The divine child, at that time, left quietly, and no one felt his departure. He went and joined his playmates of his own age in the sports and games. He, then, brought all his friends to his home. It was dusk time then. The meal had been prepared and he offered it to all his peers. The mother gave food to her son's friends with love and affection after which they all left.

8. MAULVI (A LEARNED MUSLIM)

Greatest of all, but still young in his age, Guru Nanak was playing around in his parental home but it was difficult to understand or to get any inkling about his games. He felt the presence of the Lord near him, and with him, the same way an ordinary child feels the presence of his parents around him. In the same ecstacy, he would, sometimes, smile, play or run around; other times, he would become quiet or lie down. Father Kalu and mother Tripta would be elated to see him playing around and having a good time, but would become despondent seeing him silent, glum or morose. As they were growing older, their sadness, despair and despondence kept increasing. He would go out of the house, away to the jungles and stay there a while. These were the days of moroseness but, suddenly, he would sparkle. Seeing him perked up, one day his father said, "Son! If you would like, I could take you to the Maulvi. You should read Persian (Farsi) which happens to be official/ court language these days." At that time, the Pathans were the rulers and their language used to be Persian. All official businesses were conducted in Persian. The father thought: "Let us try to teach him Persian. If he can learn it, he could become a top accountant." The brightened and alive child replied, "O.K. Dad." Mehta Kalu, then, brought him to the Maulvi.

Considering the child as the son of a revenue official, the Maulvi, with great courtesy, offered him a seat, and wrote thirty words of Persian. The child memorized them so fast in such a manner, as if he already knew them. Then the Maulvi taught him compound words, and placed before him the Children Primer in Persian. Strangely enough, he immediately, was able to read that through, as well.

After going to the Maulvi regularly and on time for a few days, this rare child started to miss his classes, and again started to remain sullen and glum. He was not punctual, and even began to cut classes. Then the Maulvi—teacher said, "Nanak! You are not paying attention to your studies you used to. Tell me, what have you learnt so far."

The child placed a piece of paper before the Maulvi. On that paper, he had written several Persian letters and against each syllable, he had written praises of the Almighty. Seeing that, the Maulvi bowed his head on the child's feet and said, "You are some great saint, who has become educated and learned without formal instruction. You seem to be directly conjoined with Allah."

The child, living in and with enormously deep love for God, again acquired sullenness and mopishness. He would keep lying down on a cot at home, or would keep sitting with his eyes closed. He would eat his food only occasionally. The parents got concerned about their son. They called the Mullah in and said, "Please tell us what has happened to our son?" The Maulvi, then, talked to the child on several topics. Tried to get his attention and make him speak, but the child kept lying down quietly. The Maulvi, then, whispered into his ears, " Nanak! The

God you love, for His sake, please get up". The lovable child got up immediately. His face became bright and glistening; the forehead was sparkling and he didn't seem to have any kind of despondence on his face. He looked towards the Maulvi and uttered a word of Persian. (This entire hymn is contained in Sri Guru Granth Sahib in Tilang Raag.) In this, the message to the Maulvi was: "O' Maulvi, you should pray before the Creator; prayer is supplication and prayer means putting forth your innermost thoughts and sentiments before the Lord."

He was explaining to the Maulvi by means of prayers that we should entreat before the Lord by saying, "We are, day and night, constantly involved with the worldly greed and avarice, and we have forgotten you. We are not going to remain in this world forever. O'Lord! Please do not pay any attention to our misdeeds; kindly lead us towards good and noble actions; bless us with your affection and love; include us among your beloveds; please bestow on us your love, O'Lord!"

This hymn composed in Persian impressed the Maulvi tremendously, and he fell on Guru's feet. Accepting his advice, he became engrossed in Godly remembrance, and started meditating on the Lord's Naam.

[It is mentioned in Sri Guru Nanak Prakash that the Mullah beseeched with folded hands:

> Kindly keep me under your protection and preservation;
> Kindly forgive me, and keep me from rebirths and deaths;
> Your reputation is higher than the highest
> Kindly be benevolent and rid me of my pains and afflictions.]

9. SACRED (COTTON) THREAD

Guru Nanak was born in a Khatri family. They were called Vedis. There are two higher castes amongst Hindus, Brahmins and Khatris. These castes have a custom that when their children become 9–11 years of age, they put a cotton thread, called Janow, around their necks.

Guru's father contemplated that it was about time to perform the sacred-thread rite on his son. This ceremony is a very pompous occasion. All relatives and friends are invited. Exotic and gourmet food dishes are prepared. They would even butcher a goat or a sheep in Khatri homes to prepare a meat dish for food connoisseurs. Mehta Kalu wanted to see this festive occasion for his son. He, therefore, consulted Hardayal, the priest and made all preparation. On the appointed day, designated for such celebrations, the priest arrived.

The priest had the courtyard washed and cleaned, and had it disinfected. The concept was that the kitchen and the courtyard had become pure, free from evil spirits or any germs. He had a large square stool placed in the center of the courtyard. He spread a piece of cloth on the stool and then sat on it. He, then, drew several figures with the flour in front of him. He made word as well that looked like 'ੴ'. It is called Om'. He also made signs for nine stars of the sky. Then he made another figure like ਸ਼੍ਰੀ, called the Ganesh. After decorating the floor, he made the Godly child sit across from him, and started reciting something, called Mantra rendering. He was thus worshipping all the idols and figures that he had created, but Guru Nanak was grinning. There was sweet brightness in his eyes. It appeared as if he was intensely happy but quietly stable within himself. The priest, Hardayal, recited some more Mantras (religious hymns) and picking up a braided thread, read some mantras for it as well.

The sacred thread is made out of seven braided and twisted lines, and made into a circular wire. It is long enough to stretch to the waist when hung from the neck under one of the arms. It was a kind of garland out of the braided wires, that was to be put around the Godly child. When the priest was about to put this rosary type thread around his neck, the child, raising his hand, stopped him and asked him, "What is this and why are you making me wear it?"

The priest said, "You handsome obedient son! This is a sacred thread. You are from a high caste, Vedi Khatri, family. Wearing this, you will become heavenly. You will be born again. Those, who are not divine, do not belong to the high caste, and are inferior and low." Hearing the last words, the child was astonished and asked the Brahmin priest, "Won't this thread having been worn around the neck become dirty in due course?"

Brahmin: "Then we can wash it."

Child: "It will wear out, and break, then what?"

Brahmin: "We can buy a new one and wear it."

Child: "Don't you have any such thread that will not become dirty nor break?"

Brahmin: "I don't have any such thread you strange child! If you have some such thread, you should tell me. Your antics are always unusual."

Child Guru: "Never consider anyone lower or inferior, be kind and show compassion to others. This should be the cotton. Giving up the greed, stay satisfied with whatever you have. Pundit Ji! What you consider the 'contentment', use it to make the yarn: give it twists of truth and nothing but the truth, and put knots of purity so that you would remain chaste and sacred. Pundit Ji! O.K.? Make all this, make a thread out of it and put that around the neck. This will never break, snap, nor get soiled. Again, Pundit Ji! If you desire to go to my Lord's home with the sacred thread on, then, in addition, you should sing His praises. He is extremely nice; recite His Naam that is spotless, solemn, pure and holy. Then the thread that I have described here will become a truly sacred thread, and remembering His Naam devotedly, this thread will build and promote your esteem in God's heaven. You are then really of higher caste and truly noble. You will find this fact only in my Lord's royal court."

Saying all this, the childlike Guru got up from his seat, and addressing all the relatives, friends and priests who had assembled there said, "What is this thread that you are wearing that the Brahmin sits in the kitchen and twists out of yarn, and makes you wear; this thread will, with time, become old, worn out and break up; the priest, too, will die of old age; whatever he whispers in the ears is unintelligible. Therefore, nothing remains with you or in your possession and nothing goes with you."

Then you wear the 'sacred' thread so that you may be elevated to higher caste; didn't you say, you will become heavenly? On the other hand, you are feasting on butchered goats and sheep. Then, you also tell lies even after wearing the so-called 'sacred' thread, you steal, treat the people maliciously, cheat them, do not remain truthful, and indulge in unclean, filthy or base actions. How could you elevate yourselves just by wearing this thread and how could the non-wearers become inferior? You are supposed to desist from any dishonest, disreputable and dastardly activities after you put on the thread. Your hands and feet are not supposed to hurt anyone; your eyes should be viewing with love and compassion; and you should have been talking sweet language. Then, you could have been lofty, noble and elevated, and then only the thread would have been effective and powerful."

"Look all you big shots! Whenever the priest comes to your house to put a thread around you, have you ever noticed whether he is making the thread productive or fruitless? He himself is not abstaining from mediocre or inferior activities but he preaches and steers others to the contrary. If you wear the kind of thread I have described above, which will never get old, nor get burnt, it will keep you tranquil, contented and comfortable here in this world and blissful and sublime in the next."

Hardayal was basically a good man. He had considered this child as God sent from his very birth. Today, hearing this amazingly true sermon from a child of such a young age, he said, "You are great. You are great. You have descended from the ultimate; only you know your own greatness, exaltation and grandeur."

All those listening were simply aghast at this child, merely, of 11 years, the kind of discourse this child had given. "Definitely, in him, a prophet has come down who will comfort others and will relieve the world of its misery."

10. HERDSMAN FOR CATTLE

Guru Ji, by now, had started to increasingly go out in the field and sit there for longer hours. If he were at home, he would sit around with eyes closed. Internally, he was in touch with the Lord; outwardly, he appeared to be listless, unconcerned and languid. If he would sleep, he would sleep for hours. He didn't talk with anyone. If anyone did want to do so, he wouldn't respond. Many people started saying he had gone insane, and they were, in vain, calling him a saint.

His parents observed that he was quiet and gloomy at home but when he went out to the fields or the jungles, he was happier. There, he would indulge in ordinary conversation and also share discourses and discussions with the ascetics. So they decided that they should send him out to the fields to graze the family herd; the family domestic servant would accompany him for the first few days after which he, himself, would be able to take charge. If he could be kept busy and amused this way, they would buy a larger herd for him.

Baba Kalu, therefore said, "Son, Nanak! You seem to be happier in the fields and forests than staying at home; you also like the cows, buffaloes and their calves and you seem to be pleased feeding them. Therefore, from now on, you should take the family herd out. They will be nourished and you, too, will be happy. We have enough at home, with the grace of God, to sustain ourselves (Implication: even if you don't work, we can pull on well.)"

This handsome child started taking the cattle out to the common grazing fields of the village and the deep ravines and valleys where grass, generally, grows tall. The cattle grazed happily and he himself would be cheerful in his own fanciful disposition, and sometimes he would close his eyes to concentrate so that he could be in touch with Waheguru. He always perceived that Waheguru was everywhere, inside, outside and along with him. He had deep love for the Lord, and he was always contented with His intense affection. Sometimes, He would remember Him aloud as if he were calling Him, sometimes, he would sing beautiful melodies as if he were immensely enjoying and rapt in fervent love for Him.

It so happened one day that this child of Father God sat down and was immersed in His remembrance and meditation, with his eyes closed. He had such a deep concentration as if he was lost in himself. He became completely unaware of what was going on around him. It was said that just as the saints would go into eternal type of conation or interment, similarly, Guru Ji got engrossed and drowned in the inebriated love for God, as if he had become unconscious. The lovable child himself was alert and in deep devotion, but outwardly, he appeared to be in sound sleep. It was at that time that his cows and buffaloes trespassed into some landlords fields, that were blooming with green and flourishing crops.

Just at that time, the owner of the fields arrived. Looking at all the cattle belonging to someone else grazing in his own fields, he was infuriated, and yelled at the top of his lungs, "You insane child! You are enjoying your nap. Don't you see, your herd has eaten away my field. Get up. If you are a decent man, then compensate me for my losses." Guru Ji opened his eyes slowly and cognately. Looked towards him with love, pity and compassion and said, "My good man! Remember the Lord. If the cattle have eaten some part of your crop, God will bless you with new germinations; the roots of the eaten up plants will sprout several times more than before; He has everything in His power."

But the enraged owner kept shouting at him and went to complain before Rai Bular in his court. He dragged with him the Godly child by his arm, as well. The beautiful enlightened faced and God-loving child stood there quietly. After listening to the entire story, Rai sent for Mehta Kalu, and said, "Make restitution to this man for the damages done by your son." At the same time, Rai, looking at the Godly son, kept wondering as to how quietly he was standing, in a dignified way, just as a prince would be standing in a royal court. How loving, serene and beautiful he looked standing quiescent and speechless.

Kalu asked, "Rai Ji! What can I do. My son is like that who does not pay any attention to any activity. People can insinuate him as insane. You, please, bring him on the right track." Rai, then sent his peons and messengers to the fields to check if they had actually been destroyed or the owner, Bhatti, was telling a lie. The messengers reported on return, "Rai Ji! This owner is telling a bunch of lies. There the fields are fluttering with full grown crops. Not even one stalk seems to have been eaten up by any animals." Rai, then gave Bhatti an angry look, seeing which the landlord said, "Rai Ji! I am not telling a lie. The cattle have, indeed, grazed on my fields. This child seems to be some prophet or a magician. He has used some power of miracle. He told me to be patient, God will be benevolent. The crops will not only grow up again but better and bigger. I didn't trust him, Rai Ji! When the child was coming along with me, he looked towards the fields again and again. He must have put his divine eye that has made the fields green and fully grown again. I haven't told any lies. "The landlord, then, bowed his head and Rai made him accept his guilt."

Rai, then, kept looking towards the child again and again. He had, earlier, heard incidents from others as to how this child had amazed the Brahmin and Muslim priests by talking to them about the Lord and, again, how he had discoursed on and prescribed the divine requirements on the occasion of the sacred thread. He had also heard that many people considered him loony. Today, he was greatly perplexed as to what was the real situation? Somehow, he liked his face very much. He kept staring at him. In his mind, he kept saying that Bhatti's field was destroyed and, the child Guru, with his magical powers, has restored it back to blooming green fields. He must be a great saint, a God-sent prophet, a true, exalted and chaste beloved of Waheguru who has landed in my domain.

11. SHADE BY COBRA

The child Guru and Mehta Kalu, then returned home. Next day, the child, again, took the cattle out to the fields. The cattle were busy grazing and he himself was singing beautiful songs in praises of the Lord. It seemed as if the cattle, too, were intently listening, because while grazing on the grassland, they were lifting their long faces again and again to look at their lovable and a beloved of the Lord, herdman.

Several days passed by like this. One day, it was not afternoon yet, when this child (Guru Nanak) lay down on a lush grass field. It appeared as if he was sound asleep. High noon had arrived. A big cobra came from the direction of the forests. Cobra is a kind of snake who can lift his head and the front portion of his face and make them stand in an upright position; it then spreads them like a winnowing basket or a hood. That is why it is sometimes called a hooded snake. So, it was a snake, extremely large, perhaps the kind of hooded snakes, pretty fat, and long, sometimes explained by some as king cobra. This cobra came to the spot where the God-loved child was sleeping. Did he bite him there? No. It went toward the side of his head and spread his hood over the face of the child (that was exposed to the sun) in order to provide shade. Many times, the cattle run away when they see a large snake but not this time. All of them came around and sat down at a little distance; forgot their grazing, and kept staring at their sleeping herdman. In the meantime, Rai Bular passed by on his way home from a trip. He saw that the child who restored the damaged field back into full scale greenery and full crop, the son of Kalu, was sleeping on the ground. He could recognize him from a distance, but at the same time, he was terrified, and said, "Alas! The snake has bitten such a beautiful child. Look, how he is lying; he does not move in any direction. What should I do? I should go close and kill the snake so that the child can be saved." As soon as, Rai turned the reins of his horse towards the child, straightening his spear towards the snake, the snake was seen running faster than even the horse and disappeared the next moment. Rai stopped forward and realized that the child was still breathing. He got down from his horse, and saw the child alive. He, immediately, brought him close to himself and hugged him tight. He really relished the feelings, sentiments and emotions, and started reciting God, God . . . in a manner that he was actually embracing Him. What Rai saw today, and what he experienced first hand and felt, confirmed his faith that that child was not an ordinary child; God has sent down some beloved son of His. He said in Persian, "You are a prophet, you are a seer. You, on behalf of the Lord, have come down with a message from Him. You belong to Waheguru, and Waheguru is yours."

12. SHADOW OF TREE

Another day, Rai had gone out on a hunting trip or some similar business. When he was returning home in the evening, he saw that the cattle were grazing in a grass field, and a grownup child was lying and sleeping on one side. The shadow of the trees had waned but his body was still clad under the shadow of the tree, Surprised and looking down carefully, he immediately recognized that the child was no one else but Nanak, who had regreened the damaged field, and on whose head, had been seen a cobra spreading his hood. Today, he saw, the shadow of the tree had receded everywhere else except from his head. He, then realized, confirming his earlier faith, that this child, definitely, had miraculous powers, and that he is really a true messenger of God. When Rai's orderly went forward and shook him up, the heavenly prince got up. He looked towards Rai; looked again with impregnated eyes. Rai was inebriated. He felt that there was love, affection and sweetness in his looks.

Today, he was confirmed in his faith that Nanak was heavenly. After that, Rai never waivered; his belief, reliance, and obedience continued to grow from that day. He accepted Nanak as his teacher (Guru), took his noble advice, and, himself, became a person who loved the Lord deeply. Guru Nanak did a lot of good to Rai in this world and favored him with a decent place in God's heaven as well.

Whenever, Mehta Kalu would become dejected, sad and sullen assuming his son to have gone crazy, or become disconsolate, assuming his son to be idle, and good-for-nothing, or whenever he would get infuriated, Rai Bular used to cajole and console him, "Kalu! This son is a gem, a real gem. He is a son of God. He is someone sent by God. We should respect him. Never rebuke him nor ever abuse him again."

13. FARMING—AGRICULTURE

Guru Ji was now growing into a healthy young man. He had reached the adolescent age but was not interested in any worldly business, chores or activities. Guru Ji's mind continued to be attracted towards the devotion and love for God. He would become mum for several days. Sometimes, he kept lying around in the courtyard of his house or out in the jungle, he would continue to sit in contemplation and quiescent prayers. [What is contemplation? If the children receiving a sermon from the priest, or the students receiving instruction from the teacher, continue to repeat the advice any number of times, it may not sink in. But, if they put their heart and soul into it without distraction, they can understand and retain it much better. Therefore, putting the mind towards a sole direction for a sole purpose is called 'contemplation'.]

Guru Ji had his full education from inside. Whatever he was taught, he would learn instantly as if he already knew it. He was in deep love with the Lord; he would be pleased listening about Him, and he would blossom like flowers talking about Him. He would, effortlessly and automatically, compose and sing songs about Him. He would spend days sitting under the trees outside the village in a contemplative concentration. If a saint or an ascetic would come over, he would engage in a discussion with them for hours about Waheguru. He would frequently talk about God with his sister. She had a complete trust that her brother, a beloved of the Lord, was His own son. This woman was the first person who had a confirmed faith in her brother, Nanak. He did pranks outwardly, but internally, he remained deeply imbued with religious devotion and sentiments for Him. Whenever mother would get angry, or complain, the sister would explain to her, "Mother! My brother is a gem, a diamond. People tell you that my brother is insane. In fact, they are, themselves, mentally retarded. Their eyes can not properly evaluate my brother. My brother remains in deep meditation and contemplation in His memory." Rai Bular also developed an intense faith in Guru Nanak after three incidents, that he was a God-sent messenger. He was not another kid, he was wise among wisemen, learned amongst learned, mature among the mature, and a perfect prophet. Rai was the second person who had recognized the reality about Guru Nanak while the latter was still a child. His faith became so abound that it remained firm for life. Rai never waivered. He received advice and counsel and the love of God from Guru Nanak. He became an ardent and overwhelming disciple (Sikh) of Guru Ji.

But the mother and father were always caught in parental tender emotion and affection in which they are hung up with 'my son', 'our son' but could not appreciate nor recognize the real qualities in him. Persons suffering from covetedness can see only up to the major external worldly comforts and pleasures. The parents did love their son but would always mope as to why their son, unlike the sons of others, did not go to school, receive education, get engaged in some business activity, and make a decent living. He should become great in this world, bring home a lot of earned money, should participate in sports, should have a good time, should hobnob with friends and relatives, and earn a reputation. They didn't understand that their son had come down to relieve the world of misery and grief. He was a child unlike regular children. He was eminent, exalted, eclatic, and true lover of the Lord. He was teaching God's love universally; was laying ground rules to do good deeds. That was why the parents became morose, sad and thoughtful whenever they observed the attitudes of their son.

When Guru Ji became quiet and appeared cheerless mendicant, he was, at that time, visualizing the world's sorrows and was always worried and concerned for the good of humanity. Sometimes, he would get absorbed in the love and benevolence of Waheguru, and would, thus be soaring high in higher spirits. But the parents, or the people, who thought only up to the point of eating and merrymaking, earning money, amassing wealth and to become big in this world, were not able to understand that the Guru, in fact, was the son of God who had come to the world to carry His message and to fulfill His mission, who would link the misdirected over to their Lord so that people could get the true and real comfort and pleasure. He remained melancholy for some more days after which he perked up and began to laugh and talk. At that time the mother and father explained to him as follows:

Mehta Kalu said, "Son! You are now growing and becoming wiser. I am getting older. You should take charge of the household affairs and give up the ways and mannerism of ascetics. Whatever business you would like to engage in, we can make arrangements for the needful. If you like agriculture, we can hire some hands to help you in that venture. We have our own land; you can supervise its farming, and take care of the domestic chores and affairs and earn a living this way. If you do not like farming, we can organize a shop dealing with the commodities of your choice. You should engage yourself in some kind of business and make a living in a regular way. If this kind of work necessitates settling down, and you do not approve of it but would like to engage yourself in some business activity requiring moving around, then my dear son; we can make you a trader of horses. You can buy and sell horses, and travel to different areas and countries. You can procure from some countries and sell them elsewhere, and, thus, make a living. This should, not only, enable you to be mobile which you prefer, but also you will be earning a sizable income. Your disposition and temperament seems to favor traveling."

"If you are not pleased with any of the above business careers, then my dear son! You can join a service like me. I can manage a job for you in this country or abroad. In a service career, you will receive a fixed and certain income every month or every two months whatever is agreed upon between you and the employer. Some of this money can be expended and the rest saved. The savings, after sometime, can become substantial. You can acquire a decent status among the folks. Therefore Son! Please tell me which business or service career you would prefer to pursue that would be satisfying to you."

Guru Ji, then spoke:

"Dear Father! You know that, one day, we all have to depart from this world. Whatever we collect here will have to be left behind. We, then, have to go to the next world. I am really more concerned with that. I keep worrying what would these people do when they leave here for the next world. So respected father! I do engage myself in various businesses that you have suggested to me, everyday."

Baba Kaluji: "Son! We do not seem to find you engaged in any business activity."

Guru Ji: "My dear dad! I perform farming activity as follows: My mind is inclined towards farming. This body of mine, is my land. In this, I am planting the name of Waheguru, my Father, as seed. I water this crop as well in the shape and form by not engaging in the kind of activity that is not agreeable to my exalted Lord and which will abash and embarrass me before Him, or due to which I will have to lower my eyes. I do not do any of those chores. This is the water that I irrigate my crop with. Then, whatever you give me to eat and wear, I am contented with. I do not yearn for more and more. This sense of contentment is used as the drag and drawing plank to level the ploughed field." [What is drag and drawing plank? The farmer, first, ploughs the field; then he uses the drag and drawing plant to break lumps of earth; it changes the large clumps of earth into fine powder-like dirt. Then the seed is planted; after which the drag and drawing plank is run over again so that the seeds are well covered over in the ground. If they remain exposed, the birds will eat them up.] So, Guru Ji said, "To stay contented with whatever my Father (God) bestows upon me, and not to hanker after greed, temptation and avarice is my drag and drawing plank. Educated persons call it satisfaction or fulfillment; then I am happy to live within modest means (modesty-humility). I do not need nor do I run after too much money; I do not have to collect money to walk around stiff necked and arrogant. I want to be humble at heart and dress modestly as well."

"Then, I have opened a shop as well. This age of ours, that keeps on declining every day, is the shop. Business is being conducted in it everyday; the pulse/breath is running. We should stock in our shop merchandise in the form of the Naam of Waheguru; we should direct our thoughts and concentration towards Him; this will be the warehouse to put the merchandise, where the business people, generally, keep their inventory. So we should put the merchandise of Naam in our thought and concentration."

"Similarly, dear Dad! We can engage in the trading of the horses. We should listen to religious books where it is written, 'Buy truth.' We can assume that the truth is a commodity of trade like horses. With truth, we should become noble, do good deeds; the latter is the expense on the horses as well as on our food etc. With these horses, we can depart for the land of our Father, to the land of Nirankar-Waheguru-Lord." "If, my dear dad! You want me to join a service of a master, that service should be for us to concentrate and meditate on His Naam. He is the Master, and remembering His Naam should be taken as our responsibility on the job. We are running after our worldly masters (employers) day and night. We should, however, desist and stop ourselves from indulging in base activities. We can consider this a struggle. Then dear Dad! This could be termed as a service. In this job, my father, we get happiness, clean and radiant face, and God showers His love on us."

Kalu replied, "Son! You have started talking about heavenly behavior too soon. You are so young. You should wait until you become old. You should get engaged in amassing wealth at this time, so that you are able to make a comfortable living after I am gone."

Guru Ji: "Respected Dad! This wealth that you want me to gather will remain here. It does not accompany anyone who leaves this world. What is, then, the benefit of collecting it? But dear Dad! What do we and can we control? This wealth (money and assets) has tricked everyone; and everyone still keeps chasing it. Hardly anyone realizes that he is being defrauded and distracted by it from loving the Lord. All are becoming its victim and going astray."

[This entire discussion is contained in Sri Guru Granth Sahib in Sorath Raag:]

Talking like this, the beautiful eyes of the loving son, Nanak, of the father, Lord, kept looking up and up. The eyes, then, got closed, and it appeared as if he was unconscious. He went into a deep trance while talking about his Father.

14. PHYSICIAN

After today, Guru Ji started spending more and more time in seclusion. He will not sit close to anyone. For several meal times, and, sometimes, even for 2-3 days, he would go without food. His face always looked bright and radiant, even though, physically, he appeared a little weaker. He continued to be in bed, once he lay down; if he would get up, he would sit with eyes closed. He had now passed the adolescent age of 15, almost a young man but his body was weak and frail. Three months went by. Then the friends, relatives and neighbors advised Mehta Ji, "Your son may be suffering from some internal ailment. Why don't you take him to the doctor?"

Like doctors today, it was the age of Vaids—practitioners of indigenous medicine. If someone were sick, they would prescribe some remedial drugs, herbs or medication. Vaids received their education and training out of Sanskrit literature. (Another form of medicine was practiced by Hakims whose knowledge was based on Persian and Arabic literature).

Seeing the condition of his son, and constantly listening to neighbors, friends, and Vedi relatives that his son was not well, and had some mysterious disease, Baba Kalu, one day, brought the Vaid-doctor to his home. He, accompanied by the doctor, went into the courtyard where Guru Nanak was lying down quietly. The name of the doctor was Hari Das. He sat near Nanak on his cot. Mehta said, "Look doctor! My son is not eating or drinking anything; he is grown weaker; and keeps lying around. Please examine him thoroughly as to what his problem is!" The doctor looked at Nanak's face, towards his feet, and then holding his right arm, was about to check his pulse by putting his hand on the vein, Guru Ji withdrew his arm and got up. Nanak asked him, "O Vaid! What are you going to do and what are you looking for?" The Vaid said, "Son dear! I am going to examine your pulse to find out what is the problem internally?"

Then the Guru looked towards the doctor with wide open charming eyes; looking gracious in his sitting pose, he said, "Listen brother doctor! You have been called to practice your medicine on me. You are looking for the vein in my arm to find out the disease. There is no problem in my arm. There is no internal ailment to my body. Dear Vaid! Yes. There is a pain deep down in my heart; a yearning for my beloved Lord's love. That you will not be able to observe. My good man, you cannot find this ache." Then, heaving a long sigh, the sweet and pleasant Nanak looked upwards and said, "Vaid! We can consider you a good doctor if, first, you can determine your own ailment. Then you can find a cure to remedy others' diseases. You will then be cured and your body will have oodles and oodles of comfort. O Vaid! If you can restore your own health, only then you can call yourself a doctor, and become a doctor for Nanak."

The doctor was surprised. Put his hand away and said, "Son! You think I am sick." The Guru replied, "Yes doctor! You are suffering from the disease of ego and vanity. It is a malady, and everyone is suffering from it but no one realizes it."

Vaid: "What kind of affliction do we get from this disease?"

Guru looked at him, again; became merciful and said, "It has distracted and separated us from our beloved Lord, Waheguru; it has made us strangers from the rest of the people."

Vaid: "We don't seem to realize this. Tell us how do we detect this disease? It always hurts if there is a disease; the spot will be tender and sore; the heart seems to be uncomfortable, but we don't feel the distress of this disease."

Guru Ji laughed and said, "O you simpleminded Vaid! See; death is hovering over everyone's head; everyone is being eaten up with its fright and dread. Tell me, if the dread is painful or not? Everyone is shuddering, trembling and throbbing with the fear that one day, the angel of death, Yama, is going to take us away. Again, look Vaid Ji! Whatever you eat daily, it gets burnt everyday; and we seek more food again the next day. Is this hunger not a constant dirty disease? Tell me, don't we become ill if we don't eat well and at that time we become hungry? Then there are numerous diseases you have learnt about. We are always afraid of them. Some of those diseases afflict and overpower us without any invitation. Suddenly, how many ailments can and do engulf our body that make us sick? When we are hale and healthy, we become arrogant; we engage in malicious acts, but the body is a prey for diseases; they can nab it whenever they like. Then Vaid Ji! We have another disease, called 'separation'. When we are separated from relatives and friends, we sob and cry in this sorrow. When husband-wife are separated, they hurt like a morbid person. When friends part company, they cry too. Vaid Ji! For how many people can you possibly find a cure? Look! There is another kind of separation; it is our separation from our beloved God. It is such a disease that people do not consider it nor are they conscious of it. You are a doctor, a specialist in diseases; even you do not recognize it as a disease. Tell me, what kind of remedy would you prescribe when you are not able to perceive this disease as an ailment. I have recognized this affliction; I know this pain; I am having it treated; you may give me medication but what kind of medication can you give a healthy person? O' simpleminded Vaid! Don't give me any medication; rather have your own self treated."

The doctor was first greatly surprised. Now he was feeling some comfort from radiation from the direction of the child; he was getting some sort of solace through his looks and he said, "Dear Son! You talk about the innermost and about the soul; your discourse is deep and hard. What do we know about these? Son! I am a doctor of only the body; what do I know about spiritualism and the inner self?"

Guru Ji: "Vaid Ji! What is the value of the body without eliminating all internal diseases? Look! Everyone has a statue like body, and the inner soul, that helps us to breathe in and out. If we do not have life within us, namely, if we do not have a breath in our body and do not have a soul, what good is, then, our body? A peg out of cedar wood is valuable so long as it radiates pleasant odor. But if there is no fragrance in that peg, it is worthless like a piece of ordinary wood. Similarly, if we have no breath left in us, the worth of the body is destroyed, and none of your medicines can even be administered. Look! So long as the body is alive, we can feel the pain; when we feel the pain, then we know that the body has some problem. If we do not feel the pain, we will not even detect any problem. In some way, the pain, itself, is a doctor like you. How about this, Vaid? If there is pain, it sends out a message. We do tell you the symptoms of the trouble, otherwise what would you know? So, I have an ache in my heart; then, I have grief about my separation from my beloved Father. Don't you have a cure for such a disease, please do not give me any medication. Listen, you simple innocent Vaid! Do not make me drink any potion meant to relieve only physical ailments for nothing."

The Vaid was awakened, and said to himself; "Is he a patient or a remedy for diseases, is he a child or a royal doctor, is he an ordinary person like anyone of us, or is he someone God-sent that he speaks such high ideals and gives such a pure and chaste advice? Is he Gorakh, the head of all Jogis, or is he Vishnu, highest of all gods?" With these thoughts, he asked, "Well, please tell us whether whatever you have said is true? We are all separated from our beloved Lord and that is an ailment. How did we catch this disease, and why don't we, like you, feel this pain? Why does'nt this severe ache, that you have alluded to, hit our hearts?"

Then, again, the merciful opened his beautiful lips and said, "Listen, brother Vaid! Whatever is visible seems all that good and feels all that nice and sweet. To yearn for all that is visible, and to obtain it, we get so involved and self centered, we get so entangled in our pursuits that we become blind to everything else. It is commonly said that so and so in pursuit of such and such objectives has become blind and is completely non cognizant of anything else around him. The self determination, somehow, pushes us far enough to attain them, then we enjoy them, eating, drinking, using them and thus having a good time. This way we become more blind. Getting engrossed in those good times, we are apt to forget our real Father. Just as, small children engrossed in toys in pursuit of games and sports go out of the house and joined by more children there, forget even their parents, similarly, we, amidst worldy distractions, are apt to forget our exalted Father. Then sorrows and diseases engulf us. Several diseases afflict our bodies. Even though the body is afflicted, the pain reaches right to the heart. The mind that forgot the Master Creator, wonderful Father, and got immersed in games and sports, had become blind. All the afflictions to the body are the punishment to the blinded mind, because it is the mind that bears all the pain. The pain is a punishment as well as a remedy because the pain hints at the source of grief. The same pain can become a cure as well. Therefore, you do not remedy my heart ache, which is a shooting pain in the love for my beloved Waheguru, but you should cure your own disease which you have, although you still do not feel the throbbing sharp pain."

Now the eyes of the Vaid were filled with tears. He stood up with folded hands and said, "O you beautiful and bright 'old' child! You are the doctor for the innermost! Kindly tell me a remedy for my blind mind, the grieved mind."

Guru Ji looked towards him with affectionate compassion and said, "Listen Vaid! May my Nirankar (Creator) awaken you from slumbering; you seem to have been hurt a little; the pain seems to have reached you; please listen carefully about the remedy: The Naam of that beautiful Father, the Nirankar, the Naam that is shining, chaste, sparkling, radiant, elegant, and brilliant is the remedy to relieve us of all diseases and miseries. When that Naam lands in us, then this torso, and the live body containing the heart and the mind get cleansed, become graceful and elegant like gold and thus get converted into a brand new healthy frame. Then all mental maladies and physical ailments disappear. Yes, Vaid Ji! Please understand that every one is rid of all sorrows, when the Naam of the beloved Waheguru is made to dwell inside us. See! Where I have got the yearning of and prick of the love of my Waheguru, there resides His Naam. You can now examine my veins and my whole body; everything is like new, wholesome and hearty; there is no physical ailment."

The Vaid, after getting bewildered in all this discussion, had become emotional; had forgotten all his medicine; he became somewhat intoxicated and was staring, without much blinking, at the radiant face of Guru Nanak, and he felt a mild, sweet, and cool fragrance and sensation coming from the direction of the Guru in his body. His head bowed down and he said, "Kindly, now grant me a boon and remove all my inner maladies."

Guru Ji blessed him and said, "You should attend the congregation of noble souls; and all ailments will disappear."

Vaid, after paying his obeisance, left, and while leaving told Mehta Kalu, "Don't worry, Your promising son is not sick; he has no problem, no disease, no complaints and no pains. He is a beloved of the Lord. He is some great soul and has come from the heavens to do enormous good to humanity."

15. REAL BARGAIN

Despite the Vaid's determination that this God-loving child had no ailments and no disease, and he had come from heaven already designated as Guru, he knew so much at this young age that many grownups and saints/ascetics did not know, Mehta Kalu was still not convinced. He assumed that his son was highly opinionated and self centered and followed only his own beliefs. Nanak kept lying around, roamed about aimlessly, went away to sit in deserted or lonely places or he indulged in idle gossip with saints and ascetics. After the Vaid had left, the child Guru stopped lying around and started to move about. After pondering over, again and again, Mehta Kalu told his son, "Son! You are now grown up and I have observed that you have become fond of wandering around. Therefore, I have thought that you should continue whirling around and at the same time make some money. That is why it is my opinion that you should engage yourself in business activity requiring traveling. The child Guru said, "O.K. Dad! Whatever you say." Mehta Kalu, then said, "For the time being you should start on a small scale. Go to the nearby town, Chuhar Kana; take twenty rupees; find out what are the possible merchandises that are more expensive in our village, Talwandi, than there. So, go and buy some commodity, bring it here and sell it. Whatever profit you make can be added to the twenty rupees. This way, after you have learned to bring back merchandise from the nearby village and sell them here, you can go to distant places with more money for doing business. You can, then buy goods from distant markets and bring them back to sell in the local market or buy them locally and take them to the distant market to sell."

Mehta Kalu, then, explained to his son, "For the time being, you should go to Chuhar Kana, about 15 miles away, buy some merchandise and bring it back. But be careful to bring a real bargain, so that there is no impending possible loss in it. You are going away for the first time, you should take Bala, a helper at home, with you who will be of service to you and will protect you as well." The child Guru agreed to the proposal, and taking twenty rupees and Bala with him, one day, set out on the mission. Mehta Ji kept repeating, "Son! Buy only real bargains where there shouldn't be any possibility of a loss, only profits."

Both of them left.

Having gone some distance on the road, Bala and Guru Ji took up a trail through solitudinal path, a short cut, still traveling in the direction of Chuhar Kana. This was a forest near the town. It was a plateau, the trees and shrubs provided considerable shade. There they saw a bunch of ascetics smearing ashes on their bodies, sitting around an ignited pile of chaff and sticks.

One of them seemed to be their chief. He was the (Mahant) abbot of all. Guru Ji went to and sat near him respectfully, and asked, "What are you and your companions doing?"

Abbot: "We are penitencing (hard meditation)."

Guru Ji: "Why do you penitence?"

Abbot: "So that we can win over all the physical temptations and necessities, and that we no longer, are allured, like the greedy people, by worldly enticements."

Guru Ji: "Are you free from greediness and temptations?"

Abbot: "It has been three days that we have been meditating, hungry and empty stomached. God will, whenever it pleases Him, send food."

Hearing this, the decorous and virtuous child thought to himself, "These people are true to themselves inside out who have been hungry for three days and having expectations on the Lord. The town of

Chuhar Kana is so nearby but none of them has gone asking for alms. If we can bring food for these people, they can cook it, and eat it. They can satisfy their hunger, and be comfortable. What other bargain can be better than this when they will be relieved of the agony of hunger. Hunger is the biggest affliction for a human being, and it is a good deed to eradicate affliction and sorrow. People also say that if you satisfy a hungry person, you will get ten times in this and seventy times in the next world. Dad, too, will be pleased that I have done such a lucrative business that will yield ten times profit now and seventy times later. Besides, my eternal Father, who has sent me here, will also be pleased. Perhaps, He, himself, was instrumental to distract me to this deserted trail from my regular route to help feed these guys. His gratification is the biggest of all gains." The child, then, placed the twenty rupees he had for a profitable business transaction before the abbot. Bala tried to stop him. But the Guru, seeing such a large group of persons stay hungry for three/four days, and basing all their hopes on the Almighty without getting apprehensive, was simply moved, and said, "Bala! Dad had asked me to do the most profitable real bargain. To help remove mental and physical pain of the human beings is the most profitable and real bargain."

When Guru Ji taking the money from Bala, placed it in front of the abbot, looking at the young man, the abbot, said, "O, you noble soul! this money is of no use to us. We have renounced it and everything else, and breaking all connections, we are penancing in this deserted and solitudinal jungle. We have thrown all our hopes on Waheguru. If He sends, we eat it. You, too, must have been motivated and sent by Him but you must have been heading towards some business transaction. This money would have been for some other purpose. If you give this money to us, your parents and the rest of your folks will be very unhappy with you."

Guru Ji then spoke, "O, you, who are reliant on the support of the Almighty and Incorporeal Father! My father gave me the money to consummate some real bargain. In my judgment, there is no better bargain, if I can eliminate the hunger of God-reliant persons who have been hungry for the past 3-4 days. Hunger is one of the diseases. What other bargain is superior than eradicating affliction?"

Abbot: "O good man, with God's flame in you! Your thoughts speak for your greatness but we are afraid that when you return home after satisfying our hunger, your father may be enraged at you."

Guru Ji: "I have to follow my father's orders. I cannot see any other deal superior than this bargain."

Abbot: "Then we will not take the money. If your intention is to feed us, then bring the provisions."

Hearing this, Guru Ji and Bala went to the town, Chuhar Kana. There, they purchased rice, flour, refined butter, lentils, and other edibles, and had them brought and placed before the abbot, and said, "Now, please have the food prepared and have a nice time." The abbot, again, looked at him affectionately and respectfully and said, "O prince, the assumer of the world suffering! You may go now and these ascetics will prepare meals with the materials you have brought."

Then, God's beloved, Guru Nanak Dev Ji, departed to return to his own village, Talwandi. After he left, the ascetics, sitting near the abbot, asked him, "Sir! This young prince-like lad appeared a soft-hearted noble-souled and God-fearing person. Why did you, yourself, ask him to leave?" The abbot replied,[11] "This young princely child who has brought the provisions for us, in my judgment, is some 'complete' person, who is loftier than all human beings, angels, gods and prophets. He is a supreme person, is the blissful benefactor, and has come to bestow comforts and contentments to the world." Then he said, "He is virtuous, who has more dominating spiritual mental powers than physical strengths; he is a philosopher and enlightened person, someone who is well versed in the characteristics of the Lord, and His virtues, and the art of reaching Him; he is the treasure house of all qualities, a mine from where something keeps oozing out and is inexhaustible like a gold mine." The abbot further said, "Everyone has some qualities, but he has it all; he has every virtue, and in such large quantities that even after passing them around to the satiation of others, they are inexpendable. He still remains the repository of virtuousity."

It seems that questioner again asked, "Yes! He is so great, still why is he going around in the form of a child appearing so plain and even like ordinary persons?"

The abbot replied, "He kept his spiritual skills, his knowledge and his virtues concealed but he has lustre, splendor, glory and magnificance that in spite of his efforts to conceal, he could not keep them hidden from me. I had detected early on that he was not an ordinary person. He is a noble-spirited lustrous, splendid and radiant man, an embodiment of Gobind-Lord. That radiance was so bright that I could not withstand it. That is why I said that I have had the glimpse; I am at complete ease with myself. We will now eat food blessed by him. God, generally, sends the food to us but today He himself came to deliver.

[11]This was written in a verse form by poet laureate Bhai Santokh Singh in Brijbhasha and not in Punjabi. He wrote about all the ten Gurus of Sikhs in the same language which is little difficult. At that time, people well versed in Punjabi, used to write in this language.

Therefore I wanted him to go lest I may not be able to withstand his brilliance."

"What is brilliance, radiance, lustre and splendor? When the fire burns, its light mixed with warmthcalled radiance spreads. When the sun comes out, its brilliance shines, that fades away at night; when the moon comes out, it has its light but we do not call it radiance or splendor. Radiance is a powerful light."

"Similarly, the soul and the spirit has lustre, splendor and radiance. Soul is the live spiritual power of our body, and the spirit in it is some kind of light. Everyone has it inside, but those are beloveds of God, whose soul and spirit is radiant and the power of this radiance, directs others towards good deeds and nobility."

The abbot himself was a God loving and meditating type. His mind was able to recognize Guru's lustre; he had also evaluated that the Guru was a way higher, much more brilliant and radiant than him and that he would not be able to bear his lustrous power for too long. He finally said, "Listen fellow ascetics! He was God—Nirankar Himself. He came to take care of us. We only wanted from him our provisions; we did not want him to do service for us. We could not endure his splendor and that is why we bid him goodbye."

16. BULAR'S AFFECTION

Child Guru Nanak after providing the hungry ascetics near Chuhar Kana with flour, rice, chick peas, lentils and other edibles with twenty rupees, was returning to his village, Talwandi. When he neared the village, the handsome young man asked Bala, "You go to your home; I am not going yet; and I would like to stay here for a little while."

Bala then left for his own home, and the handsome child, Nanak, sat on the steps of a dry pond. He closed his eyes and started thinking, "Why is there misery in the world? Some are hungry, some are unclad; someone wails at the death of his loved one or the separation of the dear ones. How can this sorrow be wiped off? O'Creator, O'Almighty! Kindly remove all pain and despair from the face of the earth." Repeating Nirankar, Kartar, Nirankar . . . he clung to the Almighty Creator within himself internally and continued doing so in the same manner a child docs to clasp his mother whom he had been missing for too long. On the other side Bala reached his own home. His folks saw that he had gone away with Mehta Kalu's son. Someone went and informed Baba Kalu that Bala had returned home. Kalu sent for Bala, and asked him about the whereabouts of Nanak. Bala replied, "Your son did come back with me but stayed outside the village on the steps of the pond and sent me home." Kalu asked "I had sent you both to bring some merchandise. Did you fetch some?" Bala replied that Nanak had spent all the money to feed hungry ascetics and had said that, as expected by you, that was a real bargain, a true bargain.

Hearing this, the father was infuriated. He took Bala along and went out to look for his son. As they left the house, Tripta, mother of Nanak, sent a few servants and her daughter, Nanaki, to follow them, in the event that the father, Kalu, would beat Nanak, Nanaki would intervene to save him from the wrath of his irate father. It happened just about as expected. Baba Kalu did find his son, Nanak, who was sitting still with eyes closed, relating the worldly afflictions to his grand Father-the Lord for the world's redemption.

The enraged father, picked his son up by his arm, made him stand up, rebuked him, even used foul language and landed two slaps on his right and two on his left cheek, and scolding him, said, "You worthless fellow! You have destroyed my house." In the rage, his strong hands were about to hit Nanak again that the sister came in running, and held her father's hand and with a jerk, pushed him away, so that the hands were also pushed away. The sister, Bibi Nanak, said, "No father, no—do not hit my brother, forgiveness my father, forgiveness." Other people, hearing all this, also came over. The servants had also come along with the Bibi; all of them forbade him; his hands loosened up and refrained from hitting him again. Now he dragged his son by the arm and started walking towards the village. The magnificent child did not say a word. His rosy cheeks had been left with welts, the marks of beatings, and 2-4 drops of tears also fell on those marks before dropping down.

They had gone just a few steps when the messengers of Rai Bular arrived and said, "Mehta Ji! Rai has sent for you along with your son." Mehta Kalu had to go to Rai's house. Even though, he was not very much inclined to do so at that time, but how could he turn down his boss's command?

When they arrived at the Rai's place, seeing black and blue marks and tears on Nanak's face, Rai himself started crying. He got up and hugged Nanak, and kissed his forehead. Patting him on his back, Rai clung him to his chest, and said, "O'God's child! Everything is yours, yours, yours—." Then he addressed Mehta, "Kalu! You are heartless; the only son, and that a God sent too, God's son, virtuous and a seer from birth! You are hard hearted, you have scarred the divine face of God's prophet with welts by beating him up. You are cruel and merciless! You have no fear of God, nor any apprehension of me, nor any worldly power." Rai, sobbing again, said, "What can I do, I being a Muslim! Alas, I wish I were not a Muslim, I would have kept this beloved of Lord in my own house and done service to him. If I keep him now, it will become a town talk—Rai has forcibly converted the son of Khatri into Islam."

Then Baba Kalu said, "Rai Ji! Look at his misdeeds. He has ruined me." Rai said, "Take these twenty rupees and don't be ruined. But understand clearly once and for all that you will never hit this child again. You tell me after making all calculations as to how much loss you have incurred so far because of him; I will make it good. You keep on adoring your money. Do you realize that all the wealth that I have got in my home is all given by him? He is Allah's distributor; he is Allah's son, an apostle of Allah. Look Kalu! The entire world is being fed by his benefaction. He deserves to sit on the right side of God. You may or may not be able to realize it, but the whole world will be willing to sacrifice millions of rupees for his name. The wealth that you are yearning and crying about, the universe will be giving it away for him; wherever he will set his foot, this wealth will be lying down before him. Remember! You are not going to even rebuke him anymore. Only if you promise that you will never even touch him, am I going to send him along with you."

Kalu was ashamed, told Rai with folded hands, "Kindly forgive me this time, I will never do it again." And he returned his money. Rai, then sent them back, and the divine child came and met his mother and sister.

17. WEDDING OF BIBI NANAKI

It just so happened that Bibi Nanaki got engaged after a few days. Across from Beas, was a town called Sultanpur. There lived a high official of the province, named, Daulat Khan Lodhi Pathan. He had an employee, named, Jairam Das Khatri. He was of young age, and robust. He was a government employee and was a trustee of Nawab Lodhi. He had come to Talwandi on some official business, and there he was betrothed to Nanaki. He was, otherwise, also a gentleman and well off. After some time, the marriage was, then, consummated; Bibi Nanaki left for in-laws house in Sultanpur-if Beas river is crossed in a boat near Goindwal Sahib, Sultanpur is just a short distance from there, and is still a living town.

Rai Bular wanted to see the heavenly child comfortable and happy. But the behavior of Kalu didn't seem to change, and he, Rai, could not keep Nanak in his own house. Nanak's physical structure was now changing with moustache and beard growing and he was growing into a handsome young man.

Rai had a thought one day that if, somehow, this child can be sent to Sultanpur to live with Nanaki, his sister, he will be happy; the everyday clashes and quarrels would be eliminated. Therefore, when Jairam Das came to Talwandi the next time, Rai told him, "Please take Sri Nanak with you to Sultanpur, and get him some easy work; both brother and sister will be cheerful together. You, too, will become fortunate to keep the apostle of Allah with you." Jairam liked this suggestion and agreed. In his heart of hearts, he was pleased that a beloved of Lord, an epitome of sainthood, would be staying with him.

18. AN ASCETIC—MENDICANT

By now, Guru Ji, was about twenty years old. He was still immersed in his deep devotion for God. Sometimes remaining quiet for long intervals, sometimes humming sweet music, sometimes uttering meaningful and beautiful sentences, and sometimes composing Shabads (hymns). It was felt as if Waheguru was always with him even though He was not visible. Sometimes, he would go out in the fields and forests. He would occasionally, also engage himself with some activity. Sometimes, he would go out of the way to help the needy; he would be condescending and merciful and would relieve them of their sorrows and griefs. This way, he remained separated inside. He would not feel any pain nor was he conscious of any comfort, he always stayed in tune with Waheguru but would never expose his internal reality, kept it hidden inside, but externally he looked like a simple, ordinary, innocent and artless person, appearing somewhat detached and sullen.

During this time, a mendicant (Sadhu) came to Talwandi. He was squatting on the bank of the (dried) pond. Guru Nanak Dev Ji sensed that even though he looked like an ascetic, (someone who has renounced the world and would expect to eat only if someone volunteered to provide food) but he appeared needy. Guru Ji saw that he was noble, but was hard up for food. He had no money and no one had volunteered any food service, nor would anyone give him any money. Then the reliever of the pain of all, Guru Ji, took off his gold ring, and gave it away to him, along with a water pot to draw water from the well to drink. The ascetic would not accept them, but Guru Ji insisted that it was not proper to return something already given away. The mendicant, then, left with the ring and the water pot. When Kalu learnt about this, he, again, became angry. He called out whatever came to his mind but the child, Nanak, remained quiet. Someone, again, reported this incident to Rai. Rai, again, called Baba Kalu to his house; he showed some anger to him, and tried to make him understand and ultimately said, "Your mentality is not changing; you are not appreciating the greatness of your son; he is a beloved of God. You consider him lunatic, you will never be able to love him fully. I would suggest that you send him away to Sultanpur. He will live with his sister and Jairam might be able to find some work for him."

Kalu, too, liked this idea. Rai, then, wrote a letter to Jairam, "I am sending Sri Nanak Ji to you; keep him with you, be good to him, and put him to some kind of work. Do service to him considering him God's apostle, and not just a relative. If he shows inclination, get him some job." In the meantime, a letter arrived from Jairam as well saying, "Dear Nanak Ji! You please come here to me." Everyone, then, agreed and sent Sri Nanak Ji to Sultanpur from Talwandi. Rai bade an extremely emotional good bye. All his relatives, father and mother also cried to see him go but on the assumption and expectation that he would get some kind of work there, and earn money, and squander away only what he himself made; but he would send some money to his parents as well. The daily squabblings and quarrels, at least, would stop.

19. ARRIVAL IN SULTANPUR

So started Guru Nanak to come to Lahore from Talwandi to earn and make a living; from Lahore, via Neshta, to a place where today stands Goindwal Sahib. There he crossed river Beas over a bridge of boats and reached his destination, Sultanpur.

He went to his sister's home who was just elated to meet her brother. Bhai Jairam received him with affection and respect. In Sultanpur, lived Daulat Khan Lodhi, who was Nawab (Governor), the highest official of Punjab, and Sultanpur was, then, the capital. Jairam Das was a trusted and honorable employee of Dulat Khan, and was a revenue official, responsible for land and agricultural produce accounts who had the expertise to estimate the expected amount of yield of grains from standing crops. Besides, he also knew other types of accounts of big landlords, other agents/workers, the local chiefs and villages and subdivisions. So one day, he asked the Nawab, "Sir! I have a young man from Talwandi, who happens to be my relative, my wife's brother, who is virtuous, of saintly disposition, cool temperament, and an embodiment of truth; also knows Hindi and Persian languages. Nawab replied,

"Bring him to me. I would like to see the young man what he looks like." Jairam brought Guru Ji to Nawab Daulat Khan. Nawab discussed several issues with him. He was convinced that the young man was honest with goodness of heart, and ordered that he be made in charge of the grain storage. He would have complete control of its operations. He, then, fixed his salary and allowances, and allowed him to draw a certain amount of provisions, flour, lentils, refined butter, sugar etc. for his use and consumption in return for his control and supervision of the grocery storage.

20. UNIVERSAL GURU BECAME A GROCER

Next day, Nawab's grain storage was put under the charge of Guru Nanak Dev Ji who became a grocer, and who was entrusted with the distribution of grain, flour, sugar, lard, and raw sugar etc. to state workers, and to the royal (official) kitchen.

Thus, Guru, Ji, taking control of the grain storage, came to sit on the cushioned seat of the grocer. He began disbursing the provisions and supplies delivering exact and sometime even higher quantities by weight. He would never deliver less than the stipulated amounts. He would store and deliver good quality stuff, and was extremely polite and well mannered with everyone.

If some poverty stricken, famished or an orphan, a needy destitute, or a widow would come in, he would give them some provisions free. Whatever he would give them would be out of his own allowance, or he, himself, would pay for them from his own salary. He would not give away even a gram of the official provisions.

The government employees and others were, therefore, very pleased with him. Nawab received reports that the new grocer was very noble, keeps everyone happy, and did not let any dent in official revenues. The Nawab, thus, became very fond of him.

Now look at Guru Nanak's apostleship. In spite of his utter absorption and the pressures of his job, he did not forget his eternal Father, the Lord, nor did he forget to hold congregations to deliver the misdirected from their sins or to give comfort to the strayed ones. He used to do his job as follows:

He would get up early in the morning before dawn. There was a small stream flowing near Sultanpur called Wayeen. It is still there. He would enter it from the cleaner side, would take a dip, wipe his wet body with a towel, and would sit on the bank after spreading a small cotton sheet. He would, thus, remembering and concentrating, meditate his Lord. Before the sunrise, he would go home; after his light morning breakfast, and changing into clean and simple clothes, he would go to his work. Before the evening, (at dusk), he would return home from his work after taking care of the official business, he would have a light snack like milk etc. and would, again, get immersed in His concentration and meditation, or he will have discourses about his beloved Lord with some of his (then arrived) congregationalists.

During the day when he would be sitting on his business seat, he would perform his duties, and when he would get a respite from work, he would meditate. Sometimes, he would mentally say his prayers, and sometimes he would sing praises of his Lord, "Great You are Nirankar, Great You are Nirankar." Sometimes he would repeat 'Everything is You and Yours, You and Yours'. Sometimes he kept saying, 'Thanks, Thanks', and sometimes would recite his own compositions. This way he was able to accomplish both the purposes of doing his job efficiently and also staying closer to His beloved.

21. MARDANA

There was a musician in Talwandi, named Mardana, of a lower caste. When Guru Nanak Ji was in Talwandi, he used to sing praises of his beloved Waheguru; he used to write hymns in His praise, and sing them, too. At that time, Mardana used to listen to them, and used to be captivated with those beautiful compositions. Then Mardana started memorizing Guru Nanak's hymns, and would render them in musical forms. Guru Ji would be greatly pleased and show his affection for Mardana. Sometimes, he would pay him something, too. This way, Mardana was attracted toward Guru Nanak and the Guru also started favoring him, treating him like his own.

Now, when Guru Nanak, working at the grain store, leading an independent life, without being dependent on anyone for food, money or expenditure, he sent for Mardana to perform Kirtan (singing of the hymns) together. (Some contend that Mardana came of his own.) Guru Nanak got him a musical instrument, Rabab, like a violin, called Sarangi. Mardana started rendering the hymns in tune and in melody, and became to be known as Mardana Rababi instead of Mardana, a menial. He established himself as a singer with outstanding harmony, pomp, and splendor. The Kirtan, now, started to be rendered every evening in Sultanpur.

In the historical annals, Janamsakhi, it is mentioned that Guru Ji was married while he was in Talwandi but in another book, called *Bale Wali Sakhi,* it is contended that he was married after coming to Sultanpur. Whenever it happened, one thing is clear, that Guru Ji's wife, Sulakhani, was not with him when he came to Sultanpur. Later, after working at the grain storage for sometime, Bibi Sulakhani joined him. If he was married while at Sultanpur, he had lived there for a while and the chaste Bibi Sulakhani came to Sultanpur.

The upshot of all this was that it marked the beginning of the married (worldly) life for Guru Nanak. His work habits, his business dealings, his divine trade, and beneficence continued as before as they used to be before the arrival of the fortunate Sulakhani. It is mentioned that when Baba Nanak's kitchen was in operation, everyone would come and join him, and, there would be regular Kirtan every evening.

22. SEEKING GOODNESS AND WELFARE OF ALL

The broadmindedness and generosity of Guru Nanak Dev Ji was extremely liberal. From his generosity, people started suspecting that losses were bound to occur in the grain business in which case the Nawab would be mad. But when the audit was taken, it would be a surplus in favor of Guru Ji. Two, three times, complaints were fabricated against him, the accounts were checked, and each time the operation proved to be profitable.

But when his father, Kalu, came, he saw that his income was transient. Whatever salary and allowances he received was spent away, He, again, became disappointed and sad, and gave him advice and counsel. He would ask Sri Jairam and Bibi Nanaki on several occasions to make him understand not to waste his money like that. Guru Ji would, in such circumstances, remain unperturbed, and would contain his father's rebukes within himself. Whenever he listened to such things, he would say "everyone is inflicted with greed, and that is why, everyone is miserable. I am at ease because I share my money with others considering both the world and the money belonging to the Waheguru; I do not squander, but show my concern for others and share my blessings with the needy."

Adopting this kind of attitude and actual action, he was endeavoring to prove the point so that the world should learn to wish for the goodness and welfare of all.

23. GURU NANAK, THE HOUSEHOLDER

In the beginning, Guru Ji, used to live with his sister. When Bibi Sulakhani joined him, he stayed with his sister a little longer but, later, took up an independent residence. He, now, started to live like any other householder—someone who lives in his home, has a wife, deals with relatives and other dear ones, works at a job and makes a living. These were but expected of every householder. Out of his own income, Guru Ji made complete arrangement for his wife, Sulakhani, would send her food, milk, sugar, refined butter and other provisions in ample quantities, would send her adequate amounts of clothings and money and be courteous to her as well. But the fortunate lady would, more often than not, become sullen. She, like other wives, wanted him to spend more time at home; did not want him to go for Kirtan every evening nor to go early every morning to Wayeen to sit in meditation. Whatever he earned, she wanted him to bring that home and save. It has been mentioned above that Guru Ji would provide adequately for his household expenses, and spend and distribute the balance on the needy and the poor. Because of the latter, the housewives, often, are rueful and disconsolate. Whenever her parents-in-law would come, she would complain to them, and whenever her own father, Moola Chona or her mother would come, she would gripe before them, too. This way, Mata Sulakhani's grouse and beef would reach Bibi Nanaki and Jairam Ji. Bibi Nanaki did bring it up with her godly brother a couple of times but Guru Ji told her that he did not make it hard for her either on account of money or anything else. "When I try to make several strangers comfortable, seek welfare for all, then how can I keep someone wanting and inadequate in any way, when that someone had been brought in by our parents, and who takes care of the household? But my love and fondness is for my eternal Father, the Waheguru, who has sent me here and has blessed me with this body. Besides, I feel pity for the afflicted and like to share my savings and blessings with others. You should explain to your sister-in-law that she, too, should learn both the virtues, to love Waheguru and to wish goodness and welfare for all humanity."

On Bibi Nanaki's suggestion, Bibi Sulakhani did accommodate a change in her behavior, started functioning under the will and order of her exalted husband, and started giving, like her handsome husband, alms and charities to those visiting them. The poet laureate, Bhai Santokh Singh wrote which when translated is as follows:

"Well mannered, and wise, Bibi Sulakhani started to spend every day under the obedience of Guru Ji and would adopt to do whatever he would suggest to her. When the blossomed lotus like cheerful faced emancipated benevolent Guru Ji would come home, Bibi Sulakhani would, then, take away the fan from the maid servant and would slowly fan him herself. She, herself, would bring in water, wash his feet, and wipe them with a towel; in this way, she would do service every day. Removing all her servants, Bibi Sulakhani, descending from personal egoism, would perform all services with devotion and love. When the beggars came for alms, (who fulfilled their needs by going door to door), she would not turn anyone away empty handed; she would give them alms cheerfully and willingly. Just as Guru Ji used to give charities from the grain store, similarly, she would be elated to share her blessings and give away charities of material goods to the needy without any grudge. She would engage herself with activities that would please Guru Ji and would, generally, operate under his obedience.

Just as a red colored liquid lying close to a piece of glass gives the glass an impression of being red, similarly, due to the brilliance and splendor of Sri Guru Ji, Mata Sulakhani, also became a very generous person under his tutelage. Sri Guru Nanak Dev Ji, being very pleased and satisfied, would also shower boundless blessings on her. He would be spending the evenings and nights at home, and the days working at the shop.

Living in Sultanpur for sometime, a child was born to Mata Sulakhani who was christened as 'Sri Chand'. The news reached Talwandi that a grandson had been born to Baba Kalu; the same good news was also relayed to Mula Chona (Mata Sulakhani's father) that he, too, had become a grandfather. The entire family gathered together, then came to Sultanpur, and had merrymakings the way the family would indulge in on such happy occasions. Everyone was in a festive mood, but Guru Nanak was wrapped up in his big Father, the Lord. He was comfortable, satisfied, contented, and savory but would not separate himself from Him frolicking in His remembrance and love; and would always receive immense pleasure helping and providing for the poor and the needy.

24. GURU NANAK'S CONGREGATIONAL BLOOM

Running the grain store, performing his duties honestly and diligently, fulfilling his responsibilities of a married life, helping and rearing the disadvantaged, and doing good to humanity, the congregation of Guru Nanak was also shaping up. How did it come about? It happened as follows: that during the time of singing of the hymns in the evenings, other persons would also come and join in the devotional music, the tinge of which started showing up on them. They were becoming regular congregationalists. If someone would ask him about the approach to the next world, he would explain patiently and affectionately. This way many persons started to follow him, and as per his advice, began to love Waheguru. They would join in singing the praises of the Lord, would try to understand the meanings and significance of the hymns composed by the Guru, would try to practice the noble principles propounded in those hymns, would start to meditate, would engage themselves only in lofty, chaste and truthful activities, and thus their character was uplifted. They stopped telling lies, stopped being mean to others, stopped being dishonest to others, and began to fear and to love the Waheguru. Several persons with such eminent and reputable characteristics came out of these deliberations. Detailed descriptions about many of them were not available. Some information was, however, available about a couple of them, the stories about whom, are briefly, presented below:

25. BHAI BHAGIRATH

There was a village, named, Melseehan near Sultanpur. A man, named, Bhagirath used to live there. He happened to be the head of the village; he was a nice man by temperament. He was constantly worried lest he may suffer after death. Just as he was comfortable and satisfied while he was alive, he wanted his soul and spirit to be similarly comfortable and contented after death as well. When we die, the body dies, but not our spirit. It separates itself from the body. The noble soul's spirit should remain blissful and tranquil even after death. This was his ambition. To achieve this aim, he met many ascetics and saints; on the suggestions of some persons, worshipped a certain goddess. He was introduced and prodded to worship an idol made out of black stone, called Bhawaani or Kali. Bhagirath had begun to worship this goddess as was proposed to him. He would sit before that idol several times a day, would meditate on her and would sing her praises.

One day, sitting like this, half the night had gone by. He became lazy and sloth and went to sleep. While sleeping, he saw a dream, in which that statue had begun to talk, and said, "I cannot bestow salvation or redemption on you. If you are interested to get deliverance of the soul from the body and exemption from further transmigration, then you should go to Sultanpur, meet Nanak, the grain dealer; he has hidden his real form. People consider him just another average man, the family members and relations consider him just another of their relatives; the poor consider him benevolent, but he, in fact, is the divine flame of the Lord, God's child, just His carbon copy, just like a son has the form and shape of the father. He has come to emancipate this world. You should fall on his feet; he will get you redemption. I cannot get you salvation."

After a little while when he got up, he still remembered the entire dream. When the day broke, he started making inquiries in the village. One of the adherents of Guru Nanak told him, "The incarnation of Waheguru, in the form of a human being, has landed in Sultanpur and he is Guru Nanak."

Bhagirath, after renouncing his family, friends and world possessions, came down to Sultanpur and paid his respects by bowing before Guru Nanak with humility. Sri Guru, blessing by caressing him on his head, lifted him up and asked about his welfare. Then asked him, "Brother! How are you here and what is the purpose of your visit?" Bhagirath narrated to him the episode of his dream and said, "After finding your whereabouts, I have come here for your shelter, protection and refuge." Sri Guru Ji sermonized him: "(1) Do service to the congregation that assembles every evening; (2) You have a noble character, and may God keep it like that; (3) You must listen to Shabad Kirtan, singing of religious hymns, with a concentration of mind; (4) Whenever you get even a little leisure during your work, make a small prayer; 'O formless and shapeless Father, God! O dear Lord! O Master! Accept me in your feet;' (5) Sometimes, mentally, you should sing his praises; (6) This way, you will start feeling the presence of the Lord inside you; (7) Then, your tongue will start reciting His Naam: Nirankar, Nirankar, You are truth, Nirankar, and the Creator is truth. You should remember that He, whose name you are remembering, is inside you. This way, you will start living your life in His presence. He is omnipresent, resides inside us; we have to remember, we have to realize that He is inside us and always with us. He is there inside us, and really, He resides there; we keep forgetting him. Let us also realize that He is present externally as well, he is everywhere, but is invisible. If you keep this practice going, God will be kind, and you will be able to connect yourself to the Creator while living your life here."

26. THE WEDDING OF MARDANA'S DAUGHTER

Mardana had gone for sometime to his village after taking Guru's permission. He returned to Sultanpur during these days and fell on Guru's feet. Sri Guru affectionately lifted him up and asked him about his welfare. Then Guru Ji inquired, "Was Rai Bular well and good?" Mardana replied, "Yes Sire, he was alright and comfortable. When he remembers you, his eyes become filled with tears of love." He also said, "Thank God, he is not being pestered by his family members and relatives; he is enjoying his divine frolics."

Then Guru Ji inquired about his own parents welfare. That too, Mardana related to him and said, "They remember you with love and affection, and send you their blessings." Then Guru Ji asked him, "You have returned after quite some time; tell me if you were involved in some kind of business?" Mardana, then, replied, "My family is doing alright, pulling on well. But, it is a matter about my daughter to be married. We do not have adequate money for this purpose. "O my divine host! You have told me before I went home not to beg or expect from any other source. That is why I am here for some compassionate favor." Then Guru Ji asked Bhagirath to come closer and said, "Take down the entire list of items, and materials such as a set of bangles, red cloths, other clothes dyed red, wedding and other clothes, ornaments and some other goods, and materials, such as Mardana needs for the wedding of his daughter." He asked him to go to Lahore, bring everything on the list but stay there only for one night.

27. WEDDING DOWRY FROM LAHORE AND MANSUKH

Bhagirath, with Guru's permission left for Lahore. After reaching there, he met a trader, named Mansukh, who had a large store, where he would conduct all his transactions of buying and selling of merchandise. Bhagirath went to this store. Mansukh respectfully offered him a seat and then asked him the business he was there for. Bhagirath handed him the paper containing the entire list and the details of the items required for wedding. Looking at the list, Mansukh said, "Everything can be made ready today. However, the set of bangles cannot be prepared in one day. You want us to hurry up and complete everything today. If you can stay here for another day, you can leave the day after, and everything shall be ready." Then Bhagirath said, "I have permission to spend only one night. If I were to stay another night here, my entire life will go in vain." Mansukh hearing this, was surprised, and said, "Why would your whole life go waste by spending another night here? Even a king will not say these words to his servant that his life would become worthless." Then Bhagirath said, "I am not an employee of any king. I am a servant of a Godly Guru. If I overstay, I would be flouting his orders. If the Guru becomes disappointed with his Sikh (disciple), of what worth is the life of the Sikh? You are wise, you yourself can appreciate it."

Mansukh said, "It is the age of Kaljug; there is fakery and deceit all over. Who is such a person you are calling a complete Guru?" Bhagirath replied, "There is a big difference between seeing and hearsay. He is not an ordinary human Guru who might claim to be complete or incomplete. He is an angelic Guru. Perhaps, God has sent His beloved presager, or He, himself, has landed here. He is hidden, and is in the form of a human being. He engages himself in business the same way you and I are conducting. But when you join him in his congregational company, then you realize that all his activities revolve around the Lord. He does good to everyone. He is always immersed in God. People talk about enlightenment, and he is the embodiment of enlightenment. I have to fulfill the orders of such a complete saint. Therefore, kindly have everything ready in just one day." Mansukh said, "It is surprising that there is someone who is so complete in this day and age. I, too, have been wanting to meet with such a complete person for quite sometime. If he can show me some skills, I would, then, be convinced that he is real and complete, and I, too, would become one of his adherents. Bhagirath said, "To see skills, or miracles from a complete person is something like asking for pennies from a king, from whom one should be asking for silver, gold, gems, and diamonds." Mansukh said, "Do the saints and the ascetics have gold and diamonds?" Bhagirath replied, "The kind of great man he is, we should ask him for happiness and comforts of the mind, that we develop a strong tie and love for the Lord internally, that our postures and habits so change, that we do not torture others. So, if you want to really test him, give up excuses and unfaithful arguments, and go to bow before him with faith and devotion. You will receive these lofty and exalted things. Without a doubt, you can return."

With these discussions and talks, they had their dinner and slept for the night. Next day, Mansukh helped Bhagirath to purchase all the required items from the market. He paid cash wherever he could get the item in question. Regarding the set of bridal bangles, he said,

"Bhagirath! You are in a great hurry, but the set of bangles cannot be ready today; the craftsman is out of town today. But I have one colored set that I had got made for one of my occasions. You can see if you like it." When Mansukh brought the set, Bhagirath liked it and said, "Shah Ji (a rich businessman)! This is alright. It is of the correct size and I like it."

After this conversation, both of them departed. Mansukh said, "Your complete Guru does not know me. But if he calls me by my real name, I will be convinced that he, really, is a complete Guru." Bhagirath said, "If it pleases you, it is alright with me, but it is not nice to test great men."

Talking and discussing, they reached Sultanpur after spending a night enroute. Both of them paid their obeisance to Guru Ji.

Guru Ji caressed Bhagirath on his head and said, "You have become benevolent, someone who does good deeds to others and does not expect any money or anything else in return. You have gone to do only one act of goodness but, actually, you have done two good deeds; you have brought someone with you who is seeking internal serenity and comfort for himself; (seeker of the comfort of mind); even though it is his name, he is not happy from within."

Hearing this, Mansukh (seeker of the comfort of mind) clung to Guru's feet and said, "I am convinced, Sir! You are a complete Guru, a complete great soul or God himself." After expressing affection for both of them, the Guru sent for Mardana and presented him the entire dowry and items of wedding purchased in Lahore. He gave him more money, too, to be spent on the wedding and other purposes. Mardana was ecstatic. He loved Guru Ji dearly before, but now his devotion and affection increased immensely, that the Guru had pulled him out of the impasse he was in. He, therefore, collecting everything and singing Guru's praises, arrived in Talwandi, where he spread his appreciations for the Guru that Nanak was a Guru, a benevolent Guru, and was more generous than even the kings.

28. REDEMPTION OF MANSUKH

Mardana had left Sultanpur and it had been a few days since his departure. When Mansukh saw Guru Ji's conducting of the grain business so very well and attending to his household affairs at the same time so ably, without showing any sense of irritation, and keeping a cheerful profile like that of a pleasant and serene moonlight, he was simply surprised. How could (or did) he rise above and be so indifferent at the time of religious congregations in the evenings as if he had never indulged in any kind of business deals? See again, he gets up so early in the wee hours of the morning and sits in a meditational posture on the bank of the river Wayeen. His body appears like an idol, in which the mind is committed as if totally immersed in the love of Waheguru—immersed like adding water to milk, converts the appearance of the entire mixture to that of milk. Again, watch the practices and behaviors of Guru Ji as well as his congregationalists; they all conduct themselves absolutely truthfully; there is not even a speck of lies." Observing all this, his mind was convinced that there was no other such a true Guru in the world. He was not a Guru like normal teacher, rather he had emanated out of the Lord Himself; he was an angelic Guru—a Guru, a protege of Waheguru. He was not a Guru because he was a superior being out of all men, he was so from the very beginning; he had been god-sent as a manifestation of Waheguru. When he was totally convinced, observing all this, he came and fell at the feet of the Guru, and beseeched, "Kindly be merciful to me and steer me, too, like your other disciples, to the path leading towards the Waheguru."

Guru Ji, then, said, "Mansukh! There are three chores to realize, and appreciate, that are worth doing:

"(1)(i) One is that whom you call Bhagwan, the Lord, and I call him Nirankar, shapeless and formless, He is present everywhere. No place is without Him even though He cannot be seen with the naked eyes. He is not visible because he doesn't have any formal structure; He is the spirit."

(ii) "We cannot achieve Him through physical efforts, but only through mental endeavors. Because of His omnipresence, He is in our minds as well. So He is within us. To attain something that is inside should not be so difficult. If we have a clean conscience, if we adore truth and truthfulness, if we keep reminding ourselves that He who pervades inside is still inside us, then we begin to realize Him that He exists and is inside us. To remember this for normal human beings is not so simple. We have to meditate on His Naam. We have to remember Him by repeating and appreciating 'Great is Nirankar, Great is Nirankar.' I have just now told you that He exists and is everywhere including inside us. He is invisible but is extremely charming and is always blossoming and cheerful. Observing something bewitching, lovable and alluring, the words like 'great, great' would come out effortlessly. Similarly, we remember and perceive Him as Waheguru, Great Guru, Great Guru. You should, therefore, remember the Lord this way; remember Him by repeating His Naam."

(iii) "We do Kirtan and sing His praises daily. By so doing, we develop a deep love and infatuation for Him. You should, thus, resolve to adopt both 'Naam' and 'Kirtan'."

(2) "Secondly, in this world, every human being goes through good and bad times depending on his/her actions. Those who have committed base actions go through difficult times of grief, sorrow and afflictions while those with good deeds, have relatively easy, comfortable and healthy times. 'Comfort' and 'sorrow' do not function on their own. Our actions get reported to Nirankar, and He does the justice. He loves us all and still loves us while delivering His judgment. When we go through hard times due to our actions, He manifests them in a manner that we can learn some lessons through them. His intentions are that we improve ourselves, and do not do misdeeds again. Therefore, we should not be nervous, anxious, agitated or perturbed during troubled times; rather, we should realize that the Lord wants to refine and reform us so that we could learn some lessons through pain and suffering. Therefore, the second point is that the lovers of Naam and Kirtan should not be bewildered or non-plussed during adversities, should not blame Him for hard times; and should consider the results of their actions and the current sufferings as teachers for reform. This is called 'accepting His will' and 'to move under His consent'."

(3) "Third point is ego, vanity, pride, arrogance or selfishness. The arrogant people tend to slide into sinful acts. The egotist shows snobbishness, considers himself the biggest, and the highest, and the others, little and low. Just as a strong and husky boy keeps pestering, rebuking or even beating up weaklings in his class, or a good player keeps pushing others unprovokingly, he is proving to be an arrogant person. Similarly, an egotist, torturing and afflicting others with all kinds of pains and sufferings becomes sinful. Therefore egotism is the root cause of sins. We, therefore, have to give up ego and vanity. On the one hand, with the knowledge, understanding and awakening that I have alluded to, we have to overpower and control our ego and not let our egos get the better of us, like we should ride over the horse and not the other way around. If you remain humble, the ego stays under control. On the other hand, meditate on His Naam and do Kirtan; these, too, can keep our ego under our holds. This way, we can ride over our vanities."

"Listen, now, the crux of all three aspects:

Always restrain yourself from committing any kind of misdeed or a sin; the root cause of all sins is our ego and that has to be controlled. This way, our character will be cleansed, i.e., we will have a pure, solemn and spotless life, and our mind will become elegant, clean, and beautiful. Then Naam and Kirtan will unite us with our Waheguru. We will, thus, be able to realize Him inside us; we will always feel that we are living in His presence. Therefore, without penance, pertinaciousness, obediency, contemplation and without renouncing this world, and without any hard toils, we will have a union with the Waheguru. After this, the Creator Himself, will bestow many more boons."

Taking the advice, Mansukh started to take extra pains and began to toil in the direction of the set mission. He continued to stay in Sultanpur. He was an educated man. He took all the words spoken by Guru Nanak Sahib Ji to heart. He had a longing that just as Guru Ji was solacing the population of Sultanpur by means of Kirtan, he could enjoy the same comfort and serenity of Kirtan sitting in Lahore. He was the first scribe who had copied the hymns of the Guru.

He did service of all kinds in Sultanpur for quite sometime, and then left for Lahore. He continued to practice the same chores that Guru Ji had prescribed for him. He would, later, visit Sultanpur once in a while for a few weeks and would enjoy the pleasures of the Kirtan and being a part of the congregation. While in Lahore, he would conduct his normal business but would, unlike before, devote himself to meditation as well as rendering of Kirtan. He would get up very early before dawn in the morning and sit in meditation. During the day, he would run his trade and business. In the evening, he would perform Kirtan of the hymns spoken and composed by Guru Nanak Sahib. His Kirtan was very sweet and pleasant; his neighbors and friends would join him occasionally, and gradually started taking part in it as well. Thus began the first congregation of Guru Sahib.

The same Mansukh had travelled to the south to Sangladeep (Sri Lanka) where he had an incident with a Raja. Later, Guru Ji also visited that place. The account of this episode will appear under 'Sadness of the South, later in this book.'

29. ANOTHER ANECDOTE OF BHAGIRATH

The above narrated event of Bhai Bhagirath was included in *Sri Guru Nanak Prakash.* Another of his incidents was also written by Bhai Mani Singh and made a part of *Bhagatmala.* It seems that both the events are not one and the same, but are two separate episodes, that actually took place. The first one was written by Bhai Santokh Singh and the other by Bhai Mani Singh. The latter incident is as follows: That Guru Nanak Dev Ji was visiting the village of Melseeha. Most probably, Bhagirath was instrumental for Guru's visit. Guru Sahib and everyone else including Bhagirath went to sleep at night. Bhagirath got up in the wee hours of the morning and fetched water for Guru Ji's bath; then sat down in his meditation. It appears that he dosed off. He saw in his dreams that a lady was sweeping a floor. Bhagirath asked her who she was and why was she sweeping so early in the morning? She responded, "Don't you recognize me, Bhagirath? I am the goddess you have been worshipping for years." Bhagirath, then asked, "Being a goddess, why are you sweeping the floor?" She replied, "Don't you know, who this Guru Nanak is? He is not a human being; he is a prophet, the embodiment of Nirgun form of the absolute and formless, the Waheguru, who is boundless. [All gods and goddesses behave under certain qualities and skills, of limited operations, and are all subservient to the Lord, who can see them all, but they can't, even though all of them are worshipping Him. As is written in Japji Sahib: 'He can see all but all may not be able to see Him!] I derive all my powers only after sweeping at Guru's door." Seeing it, Bhagirath's faith in Guru Sahib got confirmed, and, immediately started to join his congregation and to perform acts of service.

30. THE ORCHARD OF HOLY ASSEMBLY IN SULTANPUR

An orchard is a garden where beautiful flowers and fruits emitting heart-rendering fragrances blossom. Similarly, a religious assembly is an orchard, in which people with noble souls, doing good deeds, and giving comforts to others, gather together. The reciters of Guru's Bani, (hymns) and renderers of Kirtan come there and perform the Kirtan. Then, the lovers of Waheguru join the congregations as if the fragrance of Naam is being disseminated. Thus, Guru's flower bed was blossoming in Sultanpur. A few hours in the morning, and again, a few hours in the evening, Guru Ji would create a divine atmosphere of remembrance, meditation, comeliness and Kirtan. During the day, he would work at his store; even though it was a business, he would do his job well, but internally, his mind was in tune with Waheguru. One event of the time is atypical.

Guru Ji used to have a servant whose main job was to weigh the goods while buying or selling. But, sometimes, the weighman would not be present, Guru Ji would start weighing the commodities himself. It happened on several occasions that when he was weighing, he would, while dumping the pan of the scale full of goods into the customer bags, count one, two, three, four, five, six, seven, eight, nine, ten, eleven, twelve pans. When the turn for 13th pan would come, as soon as he would hit Teran (Thirteen), his face's complexion would change, eyes would be closed, and he would start to repeat Tera (not Teran) meaning you and yours, again and again and remained so continuously for quite a while. The pans of the scale were resting on the ground and he, himself, had settled down on the wooden plank motionless, fixed and steady. You might ask, 'What happened?' Pay attention to understand this, 'Teran' means, I am yours. "The mind of Guru Nanak Dev Ji was always tilted toward his beloved (the Lord) all the time. The moment he said 'Teran', facing the internally living, residing and invisible Waheguru towards which direction he was always aiming, his inner self began to address the Lord and started saying 'I am yours, my Lord!' It gave him pleasure when he said it once, and repeating it again and again, he had developed an increasingly constant pleasure, and he got drowned in that ecstacy. The scale fell on the ground and he went into deep trance remembering his Lord. Just as a child seeing his mother coming in from outside embraces her, keeps clinging to her in his ecstatic pleasure and would not let her go for quite a while, similarly, Guru Ji was enjoying the company, the embraces and the love of Waheguru."

Several similar wonders and miracles occurred. Many local and out of town people came to the Guru's congregations, received advice and counsel from him and became adherents. Poet laureate Bhai Santokh Singh wrote:

> "Many people of Sultanpur became enlightened and were at ease with themselves. They had stopped back biting; were dwelling more on equality of human beings, and they had beaten up the forces of ignorance and stupidity. Saintly people would serve them and give counsel and beneficance to others."

If Guru Ji wanted to function like a saint, then the facilities created for getting involved in worldly affairs, and pushing the ongoing congregational activities were adequate in the ordinary sense that there was no more need to do any more thinking or take any other actions. Because he had proved that there was no necessity to renounce the world like the ascetics did, and move to jungles. Living among family and performing worldly business activities, one could still become a virtuous doer of good deeds to all, and internally love the Creator—Waheguru, dearly. Guru Ji called such a person 'Gurmukh', a pious person, a noble soul whose face was always towards his Guru. Guru Ji wanted to travel throughout India and abroad to spread this message and teach these skills all over the world. He would, many times, think that whatever mission he had come for and had been set by Waheguru, he would like to go out to publicize it on the beat of a drum so that the entire world could benefit. The people of the world were perishing themselves in the fire of greed, allurement, avarice and selfishness and were searing others. He wanted to teach them the 'welfare of and goodness for all' concept only if they loved the Lord living inside them. He would then slide deep down into contemplative thoughts as to how to spread coolness and to steer passionless pacifying mission among the burning world. There, he would wait for a command from the Waheguru.

31. GURU JI'S DISAPPEARANCE

Guru Ji, at this time, was in Sultanpur proper. This town was across the river Beas, and was the capital of Punjab then. Guru Ji, at that time, was in the employment of Nawab Daulat Khan Lodhi as his grain store manager. In addition, Guru Ji had created a special hustle and bustle full of splendor by means of holy religious assemblies. We have described some of the events relating to Sultanpur earlier. Listen to some more:

There is a rivulet flowing near Sultanpur, called Wayeen. Guru Ji, very often, would go to the banks of this stream, some distance from the town. After taking a dip in it, he would sit down on a decent spot; would close his eyes and with utter concentration, worship his Waheguru mentally.

One day, three hours before dawn, he got up and went in the direction of the stream, Wayeen. Reaching the bank, he took off his clothes and gave them to the disciple who accompanied him. He, himself, went into the river water to bathe. For a short time, he was visible to his disciple bathing and swimming, but soon, he disappeared. The disciple sat there until the sunrise. Finally, extremely disappointed, he returned and narrated the event, relayed the news to Daulat Khan that his grain store manager had been washed away in the strong water currents. In the meantime, the family also got the news. Everyone came to the canal. A short while later, Nawab also arrived riding his horse. The sailors and the divers were called in; a thorough search was conducted of the river up to 4-5 miles down stream but were unsuccessful in finding anything. Finally, realizing that after having been drowned in the river, he must have been washed away, everyone returned to their homes extremely dejected and depressed.

Jairam Ji was about to start sending the news to Talwandi but Bibi Nanak dissuaded him and said, "My dear brother is a divine light and angelic brilliance. Which canal or a river can drown him? Who can throw someone into darkness whose own brightness is a beacon for others? It is some kind of a miracle, and, perhaps, bigger than the previous ones. Let us wait and see what happens?" Everyone was inclined to agree to the theory of 'drowning' and that there was no hope left; he must have been drowned. But it was only Nanaki whose faith did not waiver, and no one could convince her that Guru Ji had drowned.

Mardana, in the wake of his deep affection for his dear Master, was moving around up and down the bank of Wayeen and was singing hymns of separation. The other congregationalists sad and dejected, were singing devotional music, as well, in the nearby forests. Three days went by like this but there was no clue to his whereabouts. Everyone was surprised as to where he could have disappeared while taking a dip in the canal, particularly, when he knew swimming so well. In fact, he had saved many drowning ones, literally and metaphorically. The canal, after all, was not fathomless nor so deep; where could he have vanished?

The worldly people only know and indulge in low level dialogues. Some said, "Nanak Modi, the grain store manager, was giving away too much food to the ascetics, was squandering away a lot of treasury money and has now deliberately disappeared to cover up his shortages." It is also mentioned in the same historical annals that when Nawab called for an audit, there came out a surplus of seven hundred sixty rupees in favor of Guru Nanak Dev Ji.

32. GURU JI AND WAHEGURU JI

Guru Ji was neither drowned nor had he, intentionally, vanished somewhere. He had gone to Waheguru Ji. How did he do so? This, no one knew nor could anyone explain it, because Waheguru does not have a physical form or a body like all of us. Therefore, something that does not have a physical appearance, but rather is abstract, imperceptible, ethereal and delicate, has been explained in the annals of saintly biographies in simple language to facilitate our understanding of this mystery as follows:

> It is written that from His land, came some beautiful and elegant persons, call them angels, call them gods, the servants of Waheguru came, and under His commands took Guru Ji to Him. There Guru Ji, respectfully, fell at the feet of the Waheguru and then stood up in reverence. It is mentioned that a cup full of ambroisia, the holy water, under the orders of Waheguru was brought up; Waheguru, then directed Guru Ji, "Nanak; this nectar is a cup of my Name and You should drink it."

Then Guru Nanak accepted His command and drank from the cup. The Lord became benevolent and merciful and said, "I am with you, Nanak. I hereby exalt you and all those who remember you and your name. You go back and meditate on my Name and help others to do the same. Stay aloof and disinterested in the world and the worldly affairs, but live the life of meditation, charity, service and Naam. I hereby bequeath you with my Name and this is what should be your occupation from now on."

Then Waheguru asked him, "Nanak! How is the greatness and excel lence of my Name?"
Guru Ji bowed before Him, stood up and started to sing following praises of the Lord: [This hymn is a part of Sri Guru Granth Sahib under Sri Raag Mahalla1].
"Waheguru is consistent in His countenance; His shape is truth but He is formless."

Question: "The formless cannot be known nor scrutinized. You said not to forget His name. Can we determine His valuation with that?"

Answer: "From seers who have the powers to grant salvation or from their writings, listening about the Naam, we meditate so that He starts loving and that He can contain us in His own form. If you think that you can put a price for Him, it would be impossible."

Question: "Will we be able to know His bounds if we were to do hard meditation and penance in a solitary cave?"

Answer: "Even though I may live for millions and millions of years; I may be able to live only on air; I may sit in a cave where I never get to see the sun or the moon; I should become so disinterested in sleeping that not only the cave will not have enough room to stretch myself to sleep but have far insufficient room to even to lie down. Even then, Nirankar! You cannot be evaluated. But how much can I praise the greatness of Naam that helps us to be contained in the form of Waheguru."

Question: "Well, if we were to sacrifice our body, shall we?"

Answer: "I offer myself for sacrifice in a manner that I be tortured, lynched limb by limb, ground like minced meat and then put in a grinding mill, then burnt in a fire, and mixed in the ashes. Even then, will not be able to evaluate You; how great is the Naam that bestows us the containment in your form?"

"If I become a bird and soar in the sky and reach the heights where I am not visible to anyone; may not eat or drink anything, for which I had to come down; rather I keep going up and up through hundreds of skies, even then your valuation can not be determined but how great is the Naam that grants accommodation to me in Your form."

"O Nanak! If millions of tons of written papers are collected; with the help of teachers, if we can derive their cruxes, after which we, ourselves keep writing in a manner that our pen operates briskly like the wind and ink never gets exhausted, even then, O Waheguru, your preciousness cannot be ascertained; how great can I call the Naam that facilitates our inclusion in your form."

Then another command came that ordered, "Nanak! Whomsoever you bless with your benevolence will have My favors. My name is Supreme Parmeshwar, your name is Guru Parmeshwar." Then Guru Nanak fell on His feet, and Baba received a robe of honor from the heavenly court. The same messengers were, then, ordered to take and leave Nanak on the same bathing place on the bank of the river Wayeen and thus was Guru Nanak brought out at the same spot from where he had disappeared.

Question: "Well Sir! Tell us whether Guru Nanak Sahib himself has described anywhere about this visit to and return from and of receiving special honors in the land of Waheguru that we can easily comprehend?"

Answer: "Yes Sir! Sri Guru Ji has explained in Maajh Ki Vaar as follows:

"I was good-for-nothing minstrel, someone who sings by playing the timbrel and narrates the historical events. He is considered of low caste." Sri Guru Ji was a Khatri, the high caste, by birth; he was not a minstrel.

By mentioning the minstrel, he was not describing the caste; rather he was calling himself a minstrel or a panegyrist only out of humility. Then, he explained himself as a minstrel of the Lord, who sang His praises, sang songs of His glory and who should be considered the highest among the human beings.

Again, he called himself good-for-nothing, worthless. It was Guru Ji's character to call himself inferior. That did not mean at all that he was low but rather he did not have even an iota of ego, pride or vanity in himself.

Then, he says, "My Master, the Waheguru sent for me to His heaven." [Towards the end of Japji Sahib, he said, "The Nirankar lives in the true land of heaven."] "There he gave me a robe of honor; the robe was not of cotton or silk, but of singing songs of His praise and glory." Waheguru blessed him with Kirtan, to sign hymns of His splendor. You would, then ask, "What did He offer him to eat when He invited him to His home? For that Guru Ji says, "Waheguru bestowed on him His Naam, that is sweet like a nectar, having which makes one an immortal, meaning that he is rid from cycles of births and deaths, transmigration; he is redeemed, liberated and emancipated, and always stays in the presence of the Lord. He gave me that ambroisal Naam instead of food. I am spreading both the items, His true Naam and singing of hymns of His glory. Whosoever under the counsel of Guru have acquired both these traits, have been comfortable, happy and content." "I am saying this," Nanak says, "to adore and appreciate my true Master; that He is complete and that I have attained Him, the ultimate."

Thus, Guru Ji described, as above, his visit to the true heaven but he was not showing off his arrogance that he had become exalted after he had been to such a lofty place and to the Ultimate. It is also mentioned in the annals of biographical sketches of saints that Waheguru also told Guru Nanak at that time, "My name is Supreme Parmeshwar and your name is Guru Parmeshwar."

The Sikh's Fifth Guru described Guru Ji, "Guru Nanak was the embodiment of the Supreme Almighty-Gobind."

The Swayyea of Bhats—the verses of the bards, which are a part of Sri Guru Granth Sahib, portrayed Guru Nanak Sahib as, "That he, himself, was Nirankar and landed on this earth with all His qualities." Bhai Gurdas Ji, the Sikh philosopher and the greatest scholar of Sikh Theology wrote, "Nirankar sent Nanak and He himself created Nanak's form and figure."

It should not be construed that Waheguru goes through cycles of transmigration; He is above deaths and births. But just as a ball of gold when thrown in a fire, become fire, and at the same time, retains its original character of gold, similar type of illustration has been used by Guru Nanak as well during his discourse with Emperor Ibrahim Lodhi in Delhi. Thus, Guru Parmeshwar is someone who serves as a catalyst to connect the human beings to the Supreme Parmeshwar. Guru Ji, completely immersed in His entity, thus, acquired His form and shape.

33. GIVING AWAY GURU'S ASSETS

Have you been to a jail where criminals, sinners and robbers are lodged? All of them are put there as a part of the punishment for the crimes they had committed. But a doctor also goes into the jail cells and so does a religious minister. Both of these persons do not go there because of their misdeeds, rather they go there out of their benevolence and kindness to provide medical assistance and sermons for their reformation. Similarly, other people come to this world to reap the results of their actions and to acquire Sikh tenets but Sri Guru Nanak Dev Ji came to this earth to grant people salvation and redemption, and to bestow upon them the boon of singing His praises and exaltations. Guru's visit here was not a part of the cycle of transmigration but only a mission of mercy, kindness and benevolence, as written by Sri Guru Arjan Dev Ji:

> "Guru Ji was a Guru from the very beginning; he came down only to disseminate benevolence on this earth. Today, when he was summoned to the true heaven, Waheguru bestowed on him additional powers and strength. The command so far was to preach Naam and sacred hymns to the householder; the order was modified now to include to travel around the world to grant the message of Naam and devote your entire career for the fulfillment of this mission on a full time basis."

Thus, Guru Ji returned after a hiatus of three days; went back to his abbey and threw open all his belongings and assets for anyone for the taking; he gave away everything to the needy in his indifferent ecstasy.

Hearing Guru Ji's coming back and his giving away everything he had or owned, people gathered together there; Daulat Khan heard the news too; he also came. They were all surprised because everyone had given up all hope that Guru Ji was still alive. That on the third day, he had returned swimming across the river was simply surprising for everyone. At that time, Guru Ji's face was radiant with unusual brilliance. The Khan asked, "Nanak, what happened to you?" Guru Ji didn't respond. People started saying, "Look at his face! How bright it is. He is not saying a word and is squandering away all his belongings. He must have received a hurting blow while in the river."

When Guru Ji didn't say even a word, the Nawab went away sad and dejected. In the meanwhile Guru Ji distributed everything gratis except the clothes he was wearing. He moved out and encamped in a lonely and deserted place. Mardana, too, came with his violin and sat next to him. For twenty four hours, he did not utter a single word. Family members also came and went away disappointed as they were unable to make him say anything. His face was an epitome of brilliance and his eyes were radiating something supernatural.

34. MULLAH (A MUSLIM PRIEST)

It was a matter of extreme joy and satisfaction for Mata Sulakhani to see the return of Guru Ji well and alive. But when she heard that he had given away everything from his abbey, (where he used to see visitors) and had gone to encamp out in solitude in a deserted place, she was greatly distressed. She talked to her sister-in-law, Bibi Nanaki, to do something; he was, perhaps, struck by a demon while in the forest. The neighbors also impressed upon Bibi to make some efforts to bring him back to normalcy; take some Mullah or Pundit with you for exorcism. But the Bibi would say, "The earlier episode (of his disappearing from the river) was a miracle, this, too, is another miracle. My brother is God's incarnation. Whatever he does, is the correct action full of goodness." People didn't agree with her. Well wishes of the family took one Mullah, a Muslim priest, with them to him. The Mullah started doing exorcistic exercises and trying to prepare some amulet when they heard the following:

> "Curses on the lives of those who write His Naam and are selling it,
> Do not have to worry about the thrashing floor, when their crop has already been destroyed."
>
> [Sarang Vaar Mahallla 1]
>
> "Some said, there is the demon, a fiend, a ghost,
> Some said, he is out of tune, line or rhythm,
> Some said, he is an ordinary human being,
> Poor, defenseless and helpless Nanak."

Observing this, Mullah returned saying that the Guru was a saintly person and that he had not received any type of grievous hurt.

35. PRAYERS IN A MOSQUE

Guru Ji spoke out the next day. What did he say? "There is no Hindu nor a Muslim," meaning that both Hindus and Muslims do not hesitate to tell lies, to cheat, and to commit actions leading to sins. All these sinful action have been forbidden by both Hindu, as well as Muslim religions. Therefore, both groups are fake and artificial, only for namesake, Hindus and Muslims. In fact, there is no real Hindu nor a real Muslim.

This axiom spreaded over the town; the news reached the Qazi, the Muslim judge. Hindus, at that time, were being repressed and considered inferior by the cruelties of the Pathan emperor; the Qazi was enraged that the Guru's assertion that there were no true Muslim, was a direct attack on their faith. Qazi took along the law maker of the time, and went to the Nawab to complain that Nanak was desecrating their faith. The Nawab replied, "He is a saint; he seems to have become the ultimate prophet. Do not pick up an argument with him." But when both Qazi and the lawmaker insisted, then Nawab sent for Guru Ji. Guru Ji declined to come.

Nawab sent another message, "For heaven's sake, kindly come," and Guru Ji, then, came. Nawab received him respectfully. Qazi kept talking to the Guru. The hymns uttered at that time are a part of Sri Guru Granth Sahib:

> "It is very difficult to be called a true Muslim."
> "The mosque is kindness and the prayer carpet of Muslims is the faith."

The Nawab said, "Qazi! Nanak is weighing evenly i.e., what he says seems to be a balanced opinion." Qazi tried to put off the issue and said, "Sir! It is close to the time of the afternoon prayer. Let us go to the mosque." On a hint from Qazi, the Nawab said, "If, in your view, both Hindus and Muslims are one and the same, then please come and join us to say our prayers (Namaz)." In any case, they all left for the mosque taking Guru Ji with them.

There was commotion in the town that Nanak was going to accept conversion to Islam. The news reached the family also but Bebe Nanaki did not waiver even a bit. She didn't have any kind of suspicion even for a moment, and said, "He is above all including Hindus and Muslims."

They all reached the mosque. Everyone stood up and said their prayers, being led by Qazi. But Guru Ji standing kept staring and smiling. When the prayer was over, the Qazi said, "Nanak! Why didn't you join us in our prayers, rather you kept smiling making fun of us?"

Guru Ji, then, smiled and said, "Tell truthfully! Were you really saying your prayers or, all the times, concerned about the new born filly lest it may fall into the well?" The Guru was then told that he could have, at least, joined the Nawab in prayers. Guru Ji replied, "The Nawab was busy buying horses in Kabul." Then Nawab said, "It is true." and Qazi, too, conceded that Nanak was speaking the truth. Nawab further advised Qazi, "Brother! Nanak is standing on complete truth; it will not be proper to ask him anything else, or that there does not seem to be any need to ask him any more questions." Everyone gathered in the mosque, Sayyads, Sheikhs, Qazis, Muslim law givers, Khans, and Muslim temporal heads, were simply surprised as to how could (or did) the saint-prophet detect that Nawab and Qazi were not present there to say their prayers but were actually chasing the fillies and the horses.

36. DEPARTURE FROM SULTANPUR

Now, Guru Ji, started to spend his time outside the town in a deserted place sitting and poring. While Mardana would perform the Kirtan, Guru Ji would not open his eyes for hours together.

How long did he stay like this? It is not known but not for too long. The hermits and ascetics from far off places heard that Nanak prophet had renounced the world and had become an ascetic. They started pouring in to get a glimpse of him.

On this side, his sister Bebe Nanaki desired that her brother should stay on in Sultanpur but she was contented in his will; whatever pleases Guru Nanak Sahib was for the good of all. Mata Sulakhani, his wife, in deep love for him, was sad and sullen, and did not like it at all that he should leave home. Mardana loved him deeply; there were many other congregationalists who wanted him to stay on in Sultanpur even though he had quit his job and had become a saint, a mendicant. Nawab had developed a deep affection for him so much so that one day he said to Guru Ji, "Nanak! All this kingdom, the wealth, the command, the authority is all yours (or due to you)."

Many ascetics would come, pay their homage and were getting a lot of comfort out of the holy assemblies. Hindus and Muslims, both, were convinced that God, Himself, speaks in Nanak. Why, then, did he not stay there? Why was he speaking the language of cheerlessness, sadness and sorrow every day and was preparing to leave? Bhai Gurdas Ji has answered these questions:

> "Guru Nanak Dev Ji first went to the true heaven. There he was entrusted with the task of salvation of the world as a Guru. He received a robe of honor with proper respects. Waheguru, Himself, bestowed the Naam to him, did every kind of benevolence, then gave him the boon of humility. When he returned from heaven, looked at the world below, he saw that people of the entire world were rotting in jealousy, malice, heart burning, enmity, ill will and hostility, and were throbbing and heaving sighs of sorrow. He, then, thought that people were suffering and were in pain without a true Guru. Therefore, he put on a melancholy dress; i.e., he neither became an ascetic nor a mendicant renouncer; rather be adopted the tradition of ruefulness, a tradition against householders, because, in order to set the world correctly, to go from door to door, from country to country was only possible if he would renounce his household. Therefore, leaving the house, relatives, family, congregationalists, and friends, he came out to teach the burning world the Name of Waheguru and the concept of 'goodness for all'. Mardana was prepared to do Kirtan regularly."

Now, everyone came out and gathered to see Baba off. It is mentioned, "Then the hermits came and kissed his feet, shook his hands. Baba blessed them all with his kindness and compassion. Khan, too, came. People who were Muslims and Hindus, all stood up in reverence, and bid him goodbye. . . . Then Baba (Guru Nanak Dev Ji) was pleased and left town taking Mardana with him."

37. VIRAEE

When Guru Ji came out of Sultanpur, he asked Mardana, "Tell me, which way should we go?" Mardana replied, "How do I know, Sire! You know the future, you know the past. Go whichever way and wherever you like." Then, Guru Nanak said, "Mardana! A carpenter, named Lalo lives in the town of Emnabad; he is a saint; let us go to meet him."

Saying this, they left towards the river Beas in the westerly direction. Crossing the river, they chose a high spot with the sky as their roof to stay for the night. In the early hours, Mardana performed the Kirtan after which they continued their journey in the same direction. There, Satguru, before departing, recited an ode that meant:

> "O' Waheguru Ji! May the singing of Your praises grant me life and may you reside inside me. Yes! You be always living within me, and that I be relishing Your love slowly and steadily."

He started to leave and again said: "A Great man will come, Kirtan will be performed, and a town will spring here."

Question: "What place was it?"

Answer: "Where these days is Goindwal Sahib. Satguru Amar Das Ji, the third Guru, lived here, who had a step-well with 84 steps built, an extremely cool, pleasant and sacred spring which is present even today, and a town is still sprawling."

From here, at a slow but steady pace, they reached Khadur, which is today known as Khadur Sahib, where Guru Angad Dev, the second Guru, had his apostolate. Because of his holiness, the town is called 'Khadur Sahib'.

Reaching here, Guru Nanak Sahib encamped under a tree outside the village. In the wee hours, Mardana sang the hymns. Guru Ji was the audience and Mardana, the performer, and the trees, shrubs and fields around, sources of serenity, peace, and coolness.

When it was mid morning and was time to eat something, then a woman happened to pass by. Who was this woman? Her name was Viraee. She was the daughter of the headman, Takhat Mal, of the village, Matte Di Saran, situated quite a distance across the river Sutlej. He owned 82 villages, and this lady, his daughter, was the only sister of seven brothers. Her name was Viran Bai; people also called her 'Sat Viranee', meaning a sister of seven brothers but her father, out of his affection, used to call her 'Viraee' and this name became popular and known.

This lady was married to a headman, named Mehma in Khadur Sahib, and was, therefore, living here. She has been raised with fondling, caressing, and a lot of love, and had a noble heart inside her. She would engage herself in acts of kindness. She always wished to meet some powerful saint, a man of doing, a complete Yogi, an exalted soul but had not been able to meet anyone so far. Today, when she passed by, she happened to get a glimpse of Guru Sahib. He was sitting in his interment and contemplation. His face had an extremely beautiful radiance and brilliance, that, generally, glows on the faces of men who are the beloveds of God. But here, it was not an average man, but the Guru himself. Greatly surprised, she stopped. Looking at him, she became dazed just as a deer looking at a bright-light becomes dazzled, keeps staring at it, and forgets even to move. (Just like today if we take our cars to the jungle at night, the deer and the rabbits become motionless staring into the headlights.) This lady had her maid with her. The maid shook her up and then Viraee blinked her eyes. Then she slowly moved forward and paid her obeisance. Guru Sahib opened his eyes and the woman came closer and placed her head on his feet.

When her forehead touched Guru's feet, it felt a thrilling sensation; she was satiated with tranquility and she and her mind, of her free will and effortlessly, started saying, 'Great you are, Nirankar'. She felt some special kind of pleasing savor. Her mind was convinced that he was the true representation of God Himself; he had God inside him, nay, he is God Himself. Satguru Ji patted her on her back, caressed her on her head and said, "Get up, you the creation of Nirankar! Concentrate yourself to commune with the Lord, the Nirankar and recite His Naam." The woman had a complete solace and tranquility within her, started to meditate and repeat His Naam silently, and became a disciple of Guru Ji.

Mardana was sleeping nearby on the ground. When turned over, he said, "Kartar, (the Creator) Kartar! Great You are! Has the breakfast time passed?" Then, looking around, he got up and saw two women sitting there. He looked towards them smilingly and said, "He is the one who is the beloved of God who has set out, renouncing his own household, to give salvation to the world and to unite all human beings with the Lord." Hearing this, both of them bowed before him, too, with folded hands.

Viraee, then, signaled something to her maid. See! Mardana's inner wish was fulfilled. He was hungry; it was already past breakfast time; it was close to lunch time now. Those women presented the Guru with buttermilk, vegetables and Indian bread (Rotis). Guru smiled and said, "Come, Mardana! Look at the miracles of Waheguru! He has sent food at the eating time. You may now eat, and bless these ladies; They are extremely fortunate."

Mardana and Guru Ji, then, ate their meals, which was served by Viraee. Mardana, after finishing his food, said, "May you live long! This meal has reminded me of the meals I used to eat from Bebe." Guru Ji, again, smiled and said, "Just as the butter sinks into the bread, similarly, affection also seeps into things—love should be real love."

38. TANK OF NECTAR

From Khadur, Guru Ji travelled about 20 miles north. There is a little pond here of clean and transparent water, and there were iziphus trees around it. There was a particular iziphus tree that is still standing there. This is the one on the bank of the pool of nectar of Sri Darbar Sahib and is called Dukh Bhanjani Sahib Di Beri—a iziphus tree that relieves the people from pain and sorrow. At that time, there was no habitation, nor any temple or a tank. About a mile or two from this spot, were the villages of Sultanvind, Tung, Chativind, Khapar, Kheri, etc. He stayed in this grove amidst these beautiful iziphus trees and its fruits, and on the side of natural water. He would rest at night; and there would be a Kirtan in the early morning. He was heard singing in sweet and melodious tunes:

> "I do not ask from Waheguru any superfluous (unessential) things except His deep love and devotion. [I pray that I be blessed with His deep love and devotion and nothing else whatsoever]. Nanak is a kind of cuckoo (rainbird that is supposed to drink only raindrops] who is yearning for ambrosial water and what is that?—Kindly bless me so that I could sing Your praises and appreciations."
>
> [Guru Ji called himself the rainbird, and His Kirtan, praises and appreciations as the nectarial rare, and sweet drops of water.]

Where was this place where Guru Ji sat? It has been mentioned above that it was the same place where today the tank of Amritsar and

Harimandir Sahib Darbar Sahib are located. At that time, it was a forest area.

Staying there for a little while, Guru Ji, then, left in the westerly direction. It is mentioned that he made several stops in several villages enroute. By and by, performing Kirtan, and spreading Naam, he reached Lahore and encamped under a peeple tree but staying there only for a short time, moved along.

39. SAIDPUR SANDIALI

Leaving Lahore, making a few stops on the way, they reached Sandiali, now known as Emnabad. It was, then, called Saidpur Sandiali. It is possible that this town was named Sandiali after the saint Shandele; later, having come under the control of some Muslim ruler, it became Saidpur Sandiali. When Babar ravaged this place with human slaughter, and later the town became peaceful (full of Aman), it came to be known as Emnabad, the name, it is still famous with.

Here in poor quarters, lived a carpenter, named Lalo, who used to earn a living by making wooden pegs and stakes. He was a simple looking person. He looked coarse and rustic. Guru Ji went to his house and called, 'Dhan Nirankar, Great is the Lord'. Lalo, hearing this call, came out. As soon as he looked at Guru Ji, he fell at his feet. Guru Ji, then said, "Well, Bhai Lalo! I am here and have begun my journeys to different places here and abroad." Lalo was touched and his eyes were filled with tears, bowed his head, and then he took him inside his small room. Guru Ji's companion, Mardana, was greatly surprised. He said to himself, "How many servants and workers were under his command as the manager, state grain store, always at his disposal, standing with folded hand? Nawab was so kind towards him; he had comforts of his home; had a goddess like sister, and an extremely devoted wife who was doing enormous service; he left them all. On the way, he was pampered and revered. Where has he landed today? A carpenter who is good only to make pegs and stakes! Who does not have a cot, a stool, sheets or even durees to sit on or lie down."

In the meantime, Lalo went out and brought something like a small cot and had Guru Ji seated on it. For quite a while, there was no exchange of any words between them. Then Lalo, on one side outside, started preparing the food. Inside, Mardana asked Guru Ji, "Sire! Who is this man where you have come walking all the way? Leaving your own home, living on the outskirts of the town, where have you come to?" Guru Ji smiling said, "We have come to the home of 'devotion,'

Mardana! Where work ethics are honest and lofty; at the same time, the mind is enlightened, alert, sensitive and conscious, and is immersed in the spirituality of the Lord."

The food was ready. Lalo came and asked them, "Kindly come to the kitchen to eat." [kitchen was supposed to be a clean and chaste place.] Sri Guru Ji said, "Lalo! The entire world is the 'kitchen' and when inbued in 'truth', it becomes chaste. You, please bring the food right here." When Lalo brought roti (bread) out of course grains, and greens, Mardana said to himself, "Where have we come, the dry bread and my throat? Well! whatever Guru's wish, that is acceptable to me. O mind, eat and eat with pleasure." With these thoughts, he had the food but to his surprise, it tasted sweet and palatable like the nectar. When Satguru also finished eating, Lalo's meditational and disciplined instinct was impregnated in unshaken spiritual blissfulness. Previously, he used to work hard toward this, but now the devotion of Waheguru gave him pleasure naturally, and his mind pervaded in semi-intoxicated sweetness.

40. MILK OR BLOOD

It had been about three days since they had been staying in this small structure, nay, a hut, when Sri Guru Ji started to get ready. But Lalo stood before him with folded hands, with eyes filled with emotional tears, and said, "Please do not go so soon; stay for a few days more; give me your glimpses for a little longer." Sri Guru Ji, seeing his utter devotion and affection, decided to stay for a few more days. The routine developed as follows: 'Guru Ji would go out early in the morning; there he would sit cross legged either on a small terrace of stones or a small base of sand; people call this meditational penance. But the Guru Ji was not only doing physical penance, but he was sitting in deep affectionate trance and meditating on the Naam of Waheguru.

It became known in the town that a Vedi Khatri was doing extremely hard self mortification, and penance; he did not eat nor drink. He would eat four or five leafbuds of calotropis growing in there and go on for hours in his concentrational meditation; would keep sitting in one place, and his interment would not be broken; at the same time, people would say "Being a Vedi, he is staying with a carpenter, a man of low caste; besides, he keeps with him a Muslim bard." If Mardana were to go to the market for some errands, people would ridicule him and say, "There goes the bard of the aberrant and the misdirected who is mixing high castes with menials."

Thus, after a few days, Mardana, taking permission, left but Guru Ji continued to stay there. The place where Guru Ji used to sit in tune with Waheguru in deep meditation is today known as Rorhi (stones) Sahib, near which is a memorial tank as well. There lies Bhai Lalo's well as well, near the homes of Diwans. It is not clearly known how the government of Pakistan is taking care of this Gurdwara, since Partition.

Guru Ji remained there for quite a while. Some people would, occasionally, gather together and received Sikh education. One day, a few Brahmins (of so called learned and priestly caste) came to make him understand that he should be conscious of the castes; and that he, himself, belonged to the high caste of Orators of Vedas, Vedi. But became answerless before Guru's responses. Finally, people started calling him 'Nanak Tapa, the self mortificator', and many Muslims 'Nanak Shah'. [Shah, literally means rich trader, but Muslim refer it to Sufi, a saint]. The average persons came from far and near places, and enjoyed the holy assemblies but the Hindu and Muslim priests (Brahmins and Mullahs) started to get a little annoyed, because both these classes started considering him a threat to their congregations. If everyone went to his holy assemblies, who would come to theirs?

The ruler of Emnabad was Pathan Khan; he was like a Raja and Malik Bhago was his chief official (agent). The Mullahs started back-biting and tale bearing against Guru Ji before the Khan and the Brahmins before the Malik. They made other efforts so that Guru Ji should leave the place. The day came when Malik Bhago had organized a big feast to feed the Brahmins with Mahalpure, like rich pancakes, Puris, the fired bread, Khir, the rice pudding and stuffed fried cakes etc. Therefore, invitations were sent by Malik Bhago to all saints, and ascetics. The Brahmins, out of shear jealousy invited Guru Ji as well; they knew that the Malik would be angry if he did not show up. It happened as expected. Guru Ji did not come to his house for the feast. Then, the Brahmins told tales to the Malik, 'Look Malik! How arrogant is Nanak Tapa? He has the audacity to decline your invitation. Malik Bhago became mad. He sent a Brahmin again. "Go and fetch him before me." But when the Brahmin reached Guru Ji, he told him, "I am a mendicant, and I have no business with princes and officials." When Guru Ji didn't come, the back stabbers incited the Malik more. Malik, then, sent five Brahmins and told them that if he still refuses to come, arrest him and bring him here. Guru Ji, hearing the orders and the options, smiled and came along. When he reached there, people had gathered around the Malik. Guru Ji went in and stood there quietly somewhere in the back. Malik, then said, "O Tapa! You have been eating food in the homes of menials, the low caste people, and refuse to come to clean and chaste feast of the Brahmins (the high caste people). Then you deal with low caste bards, and show hatred for us, the Khatris, the high caste, the same as yours. What is this?" Guru Ji replied, "I am a mendicant of the Lord, and I eat whatever, whenever and from wherever He gives." The Malik said, "Then, you could have eaten from my gala feast as well." Guru Ji smiled and said, "O.K. Malik Ji! Get some of your foods, fried cakes etc." and, at the same time, told Lalo "You go and bring some of the left overs, the dry and course bread from your home." When both arrived, then Guru Ji held, in his right hand Lalo's dried and stale bread, and in the other Malik Bhago's (so called) fresh, rich and high taste Puris and stuffed cakes etc.; stretched his arms out, squeezed both of his hands. See what happened; milk drops started falling from the dried bread and blood drops came out of the so called rich, clean and chaste food. Seeing this, the entire assembly which included people from all over the town, were greatly surprised, and were all terrified that this Tapa was very powerful and full of skills. They became awestruck of his mystical powers. Malik got infuriated that he had been insulted before the entire gathering and chagrined as well. Guru Ji said, "Look Malik! The seed of the acacia tree has no thorns but when the seed germinates, and becomes a shrub, the thorns come out. Similarly, the grand food out of the income of force, coercion, cruelty, sins, and irreligious actions may be savory to eat for the average person but if eaten by saints and mendicants becomes painful. That is why the feasts prepared by monies earned with absolutism, and subjection is forbidden for the religious souls, and those giving such foods in alms and charities do not draw any benefits out of them either. Rather, they are punished for the misdeeds and sinful actions by which they had collected the wealth." Saying this, Guru Ji came out of Malik's home and went to the mud hut of Bhai Lalo.

In this episode, Guru Ji has taught us to make an honest living, live within your honestly earned means, share it with others, and give charity; this will bear fruits; the donations will give contentment and comfort in this as well as the next world.

41. RELEASE OF ASCETICS

Another incident happened in Emnabad. The son of the ruler, and the garrison commander of Sandiali, the Khan, got ill. He, then, one day, asked Malik Bhago, "My young son is not getting well; he is deteriorating by the day, and no medication or cure are being effective."

Bhago advised him, "The prayers of saints is very powerful, i.e., if some 'complete' seer would come and pray for your son, he will get well but he has to be only a 'complete' saint." 'Complete' is someone who should be truly a beloved of the Lord but people consider someone 'complete' who has miraculous powers and should be able to display his miracles. The Khan asked Bhago, "Who you think is a complete saint? How do I recognize him?" Then Bhago replied, "Arrest all those ascetics who are around and tell them that you would release them only after they cured your son. Anyone who is complete will, automatically, show his miracles." The Khan, on the basis of the information and names given by Bhago, had all the saints arrested and brought before him. Guru Nanak whose name had also been supplied by Bhago, was also brought the same way.

All saints, mendicants and ascetics brought, at the instance of the Khan, were sitting there. Lalo, when he heard about all this, came down running, seeing the world's shackle breaker in chains himself, he cried, "This world consists of fools which is enemical to and tortures the exalted persons who are, in fact, themselves a source of solace and comfort."

Guru Ji then said, "Lalo! Do not be emotional. Watch the actions of the Creator. This is, perhaps, one of His mystic acts."

Nawab had, by now, arrived. He addressed them all, "Lovers of Allah! Please cure my ailing son. Say prayers of benevolence, welfare, and health, i.e., kindly say prayers so that my son becomes healthy again." Everyone kept quiet but Guru Ji spoke, "Listen Khan! Have you ever seen grapes on an acacia tree?" Nawab replied, "No." Guru Ji spoke, again, "How can there be a fruit of 'welfare and health' to force and coercion? i.e., You are expecting that these noble souls should be instrumental for your son's recovery while you are imposing so many cruelties on them. You have hurt their feelings, and how do you expect the welfare and health (for your son) to sprout out of their tortured minds?"

After he heard these sentences, the Nawab began to think, "Perhaps, this saint seems to be correct in his assessment. For the sake of his attachment to his son, he became humble, subdued and penitent and said, "Kindly be merciful and compassionate, men of God!" Guru Ji, then, said, "Khan! Let, whatever is going to happen under His will, take place." Khan became more subdued, asked for forgiveness and said, "O' men of God! Kindly pardon my transgressions but heal my son of his afflictions."

Guru Nanak Dev Ji was a master of miracles but would never exhibit his powers. He kept thinking at that time that this stupid Khan was being so unfair and cruel on all those ascetics; I should, first, have them set free; many of them were men of meditation and prayers but all were innocent. It was within the Will of Waheguru to have some of his beloved worshipping saints being agonized, liberated; this deed would get the happiness and blessings of the Lord; He loves all His saints. He, then, closed his eyes for a while and then opened up and said, "The recovery of your son lies in the leftover crumbs of food of the ascetics." Khan said, "Do whatever you have to; kindly cure him."

Then Guru Ji told Lalo, "Go and fetch some stale orts of food from your home." Lalo went and brought them and those bits of food were given to the son of the Khan. He ate, and with Guru's blessing, he was cured. Nawab was nonplussed seeing this miracle. "How powerful is this saint." Standing nearby was Bhago, who was surprised, confused and nervous and was trembling with terror. The entire assembly was wonder struck, and all the captured saints were simply astonished.

Malik Bhago fell on Guru's feet the following day, "I have committed disobedience and solecism; kindly forgive me." Guru Ji, then, said, "My disobedience? Nanak's solecism? No! There is no defiance of Nanak. You should be terrified of the defiance and disrespect that you have committed on yourself and the public, and that you are committing against the Lord. Look! The birds and animals roam around all day in search of food as if they are working hard to feed themselves; they soar high in the sky, always healthy and happy. Food earned honestly and with hard work is always consoling and contenting. Hard work keeps the body fit; labor and toil facilitates in the path towards the Lord. To snatch someone elses assets forcibly, take it away by fraudulent means, thus amassing your own wealth, and then to sit on it like a snake, is a physical affliction, a mental disease, and a spiritual malady. Look! You have lost your own self; you have parted company with yourself; you have killed your own self; take pity on yourself, revive your dead self respect back to life and inject a drop of religion, honesty and compassion in it." Guru Ji was telling him that he had become malicious by tyrannizing others, his mind had become wicked and evil, as if he had become afflicted and dead.

Bhago: "Sire! The mind has an emotional fit; whatever you say is palatable but kindly tell me how can I, with this bony body and lazy and lethargic disposition, developed over the periods, labor harder?"

Satguru: "The management of the royal throne is labor; the carrying of basket on the head by the poor is labor; the scale of the shop keeper is labor only if keeping an eye towards the Lord, everyone does his/her own chores honestly. Your duty is to work hard to earn a living, but only if you do recognize others' rights, do justice to others, do not take any kind of bribe, and do not tyrannize or coerce others. Yes! All chores, responsibilities, and activities are well only if they are conducted in a noble and honest manner. Whether we have acquired an occupation, or we have been entrusted with certain businesses, contrition and pentinence kill the truth and the strength of all occupations. If there is no attrition or compunction, then the load (basket) of a laborer, the scales of the grocer, the order of the commander, just acts by the king, and the donation of noble thoughts liberally by the saints are all honest work. All this becomes a part of meditation if we keep the Lord in our hearts and whatever we do, whatever is our share, whatever has been entrusted on us by the destiny or by His choice or kindness, we stay contented within them. If some farmer, after putting his blood and soul in his farming, and paying the high revenues to the state officials, is left with bare minimum for his livelihood, and to snatch away even that from him or someone else with force, or to terrorize or tyrannize a trader of nobility and religion (saint), is tantamount to blood squeezing. Just as the blood of an animal can be drained by chopping of its head, similarly, to deprive someone of his honest earnings oppressively, and to do so dishonestly and fraudulently is blood sucking."

Hearing sentences like these, Bhago fell on Guru Ji's feet, and became Guru's disciple. He gave away all his wealth amassed through bribes. He pledged to become a noble soul henceforth. He began to remember His Naam, started to meditate, began to do justice to others, and to make an honest and rightful living. It is mentioned in *Bala's Janam Sakhi* (Biographies of Saints) that the Guru was pleased with the drastic change and the humility in Bhago's life, and said, "Bhago! May you be blessed and exalted." It is also mentioned in the same *Janam Sakhi* that the Khan (Nawab) came and fell on Guru's feet, and begged for forgiveness. Guru Ji, then, said, "You Khan and Bhago! Both should go and seek the pleasures of all the captured saints."

Both of them went and asked all the saints for their pardon. All of them were let go respectfully. We should say, "Great is Guru Nanak" who had all of them redeemed from undeserving captivity, and who had, thus, made them happy.

One day after this episode, Mardana returned. Guru Ji, getting the news about the yearning of Rai Bular and other messages brought by Mardana, departed towards Talwandi. Bhai Lalo very much liked him to stay on longer but Guru Ji, acquiring the form of benefactor wind, had assumed the task of going from door to door, place to place and country to country, comforting the humanity.

42. GURU'S RETURN TRIP TO TALWANDI

Sri Guru Nanak Dev Ji left Saidpur Sandiali. Lalo had tears in his eyes and supplicated with folded hands, "You are leaving so soon." Satguru Ji looked at him with love and kindness and said, "I shall return." Thus, he bade good bye and departed.

Guru Ji and Mardana began their trek progressing gradually, making a few stops enroute, meeting certain persons, and putting them on the correct path leading towards the Lord, arrived in Talwandi in about ten days, and encamped near a well outside the town. The news went around that some saint had landed near the well. It was later confirmed that it was no one else but, Nanak, the recluse son of Mehta Kalu. The news reached his home as well. Guru's mother came in a hurry. Afterwards his father Kalu and uncle Lalu also came. Seeing his mother arriving, Guru Ji had just gotten up that his mother hugging his divine head to her neck, cried and sobbed with deep love. Then he met with his father and uncle. Uncle Lalu, then, signaled Kalu not to say anything lest he may say something unsavory. The mother tried to persuade him to come home. Then Lalu tried to induce him to agree to go home. Guru Ji replied, "I have now occupied the home of true Father." Lalu thought, "Our suggestion appears hard for him to swallow; he may not agree to our proposal but if we take him to Rai Bular whom he loves so dearly, he might agree to his advice." Lalu, then said, "Since you have come here, why don't you go to meet Rai; he has been longing to see you." In fact, Guru Ji had come there on Rai's invitation just to see him. He got up and started walking towards Rai's home. Rai was sitting on a cot. He immediately got up but Guru Ji, quickly, held him. Rai made him sit toward the head of the cot and himself sat on the foot of the cot, a symbol of respect and reverence. Tears kept trickling down from the eyes of Rai for quite some time and Guru Ji kept looking at him with kindness and benevolence. Rai, then, said, "O You the bestowed one! Get me forgiveness and salvation from the Lord."

Guru Ji: "Rai Ji! You have been blessed from the very beginning. You have been granted forgiveness right from the Lord's heaven."

Rai: "If I have been granted forgiveness from the beginning, you, kindly, show your own beneficence as well."

Guru Ji: "Rai Ji! You will be wherever I shall be."

Rai: "Kindly allow me to touch my head on your feet, thus fulfilling my long cherished desire."

Saying this, Rai got down quickly from the cot and placed his head on Guru Ji's beautiful feet. As soon as Rai's head touched his feet,

Rai's mind which had lodged in its emotional love and despair of separation, suddenly had a sensation of cheerfulness and every limb of his body was thrilled and blossomed.

'Nanak says, the dedicated ones are always blossoming.' Rai attained the 'spiritual flowering', the end result of true meditation. With the advent of such a blooming, the transgressions and their sorrowful results are wiped off.

> 'Who listens to the Naam would have their sins and sorrows erased'
> When the pain and the distress fall off, then,
> 'Nanak says, the dedicated ones blossom forever.'

After staying in this stage of ecstasy for sometimes, Rai asked his servant to tell Sudha Brahmin to prepare the food. Everyone would be eating here today.

Seeing so much affection and love for Rai, the family requested Rai to impress upon Nanak not to go away. He should stay home even if he would like to be in a posture of hard meditation, and dress up like a recluse. Rai asked Guru Ji, "You may practice ascetism but kindly keep on staying here. All the land that I own is yours. The tillers will till the land, you distribute and share the output with others; do whatever pleases you; no one will question your activities."

Guru Ji said, "Farming, conducting business sitting in a store, trading and working extremely hard with a determined mind and performing service, in all these phases, I have remembered the Naam of my Master. In fact, meditation of His Naam includes everything, farming, trading, business, service etc. Rai Ji! All this is in His will, and under His command." Rai was a man of 'obedience and consent'. He understood quickly that the Guru was imbued with and immersed in deep love and dedication for the Master. In His devotion, he has become a mendicant to grant salvation to the world. To stop him from doing so would be equivalent to 'interfering with His Will'. Then Rai said, "Please tell us if you have any other command that you will want us to accept to follow." Guru Ji said, "Here is the command:

> Do only those acts which please Him; Remember only Him; Whenever and wherever, you become helpless, worship the Master, and seek and stay under His protection; with folded hands, bow before Him and accept His refuge."

It is also written that one day when Guru Ji got up in the early morning for his bath, he learnt that there was no running well. He casually said, "There is no pond here?" When Rai came to know about this, he immediately had the ground excavated there and had it filled with clean water.

43. TULSAN, THE MAID

Guru Ji remained in Talwandi for some time but would spend his nights only under the shades of the trees. During the day, he would walk around here and there; sometimes, he would go to Rai to bless him; but he would, mostly, eat his meals with his mother who would prepare and present the food with utmost affection. When the family became almost certain that he was not going to stay at home but was about to leave them anytime, they had reconciled to the idea that he should stay in town for as long as possible. One day, when Guru Ji came home, Mata Ji (mother Tripta) was cooking food. Guru Ji lay down on a cot in the courtyard, and appeared to have fallen asleep. When the food was ready, (which amongst the Sikh families is termed Prasad, the food offered to the Lord), Sri Mata Ji told her maid servant, Tulsan, to go and tell her darling son that it was time to eat. Tulsan was an attendant to Mata Ji. She was extremely well disposed by temperament and was faithful. When she went, she saw Guru Ji lying with his face up with eyes closed, and his face overflowed and deluged in some supernal and divine beauty. Tulsan did not consider it proper to call out to wake him up, and, instead, touched his feet. As soon as she touched Guru Ji's feet, Tulsan felt a strange sensational thrill and an unusual affection within her. She kissed the feet and then held them in her hands. Soon afterwards, she reposed and went into a trance. There she saw that a ship was about to sink; the captain-owner, who had merchandise worth millions on it, was sobbing and screaming, 'Guru Nanak, Guru Nanak' and was praying, "O Guru Ji! Kindly reach me and save me and my ship." What Tulsan saw then was unbelievable to her. She saw that Guru Ji reached there and saving the ship steered it safely towards the shore. Seeing all this, Tulsan went to her mistress and said, "Mata Ji! Dear son is asleep."

Mata Ji told her to go back and wake him up. The food would get cold. Tulsan, then, said, "He is busy saving the ship of his disciple from sinking in deep oceans and taking it safely towards the shores. Let him be free, and I will, then, wake him up." Mata Ji thought that since her son had become a recluse, the maid was, perhaps, tacitly chiding her. She, herself, went, woke her son up, brought him to the kitchen and served the food affectionately. When he finished eating, rinsed his mouth and came to take his seat, Mata Ji said, "Look, my darling son!

You should not adopt this guise of an ascetic; you should have a beautiful home like many other people and become a person of social status so that you become a respectable member of the community, and people extend similar respect to us as well. Now people are laughing at us. What to talk of others, even our own maid had the audacity to be sarcastic, to make fun of us."

Sri Guru Ji: "Mother dear! Has someone talked to you today disrespectfully?"

Mata Ji said, "See this Tulsan, an attendant in our house! She was sent to wake you up. She returned and said that the dear son was saving sinking ships in the ocean."

Satguru smiled and said, "Mother dear! Do not pay attention to Tulsan. Do not take her words seriously, nor should you get angry with her. She is nearly crazy. We shouldn't mind words spoken out by insane people."

Guru Ji said in a casual manner, but his spiritual power was so strong that Tulsan, actually, became lunatic. It is written that Tulsan remained half mad, but when she passed away, she received redemption, went straight to the Waheguru and remained there forever. From this emancipation from corporeal existence, it can be understood that Tulsan had not really become mad, but she appeared from outside in an intoxicated carefree state. Inside, however, she was in link with the Waheguru. Outwardly she gave an impression only that she was not in complete control of her faculties. This was not quite true. She did not have any other physical ailment, discomfort or pain nor was her ecstatic state any kind of disease or affliction.

44. RETURN TO SAID PUR

Guru Ji started preparing his departure from Talwandi. Rai did not want him to leave; he became emotional on the thought of impending separation; his eyes would become filled with tears and he would feel some strange tension in his heart. Rai was old now and afraid that if the Guru went abroad, he would be unable to see him again in his lifetime. He was, therefore, greatly saddened. But Guru Ji gave him such sermons that he was strengthened internally so much that he became confident, and comfortable in his own inner self. Guru Ji had redeemed him of corporeal existence and transmigration, that after death, he would go straight to the land of Waheguru and remain there. He would not return to this world and would stay happy both here and there. It is mentioned that Guru Ji became merciful and benevolent to Rai and blessed him.

Guru Ji, then, came home; gave such a sermon and advice to his parents that they, too, became self comfortable. He left Talwandi for Said Pur for Lalo. When he arrived there, Lalo was simply elated to see Guru Ji again. He met and received him with utmost respect and affection and performed all kinds of service. Guru Ji stayed there for a few days; many other people whom Guru Ji had redirected towards noble goals and good deeds also came to see him and were comforted. Guru Ji, then departed from there as well but he had bestowed upon Lalo the love for the Lord and blessed him before leaving. Lalo, in tune with Waheguru, while meditating and remembering Him, became a saint.

The following places have been in existence in memory of Satguru for a long time:

(1) WELL OF BHAI LALO: This well used to be in Bhai Lalo's courtyard, where Guru Ji used to sit during his visit there.

(2) RORHI SAHIB: This is the spot, where Guru Ji, sitting on a small terrace of stones, used to do devotional worship (penance). This spot is about 8 miles from Emnabad in the south westerly direction.

(3) CHAKKI SAHIB: Here, the same grinding mill is preserved which was given to him to grind flour when captured along with other people of the town, and it used to rotate of its own. This news reached the cruel monarch; the Guru Ji was instrumental in having all the prisoners freed.

[It is not clearly known how these sacred places are being preserved and managed by the Pakistan government these days. Emnabad is a part of District Gujranwala in Pakistan.]

45. THE STORY OF HARRAPPA

Guru Ji left Said Pur in the southerly direction, and reached Lahore, stayed there for a few days and went through quickly. After this, he did not stay in any habitation; kept walking in outer areas and deserted places; and would spend the nights under the trees. If he reached some village or town, he would stay outside the hamlets. He would ask Mardana, "Are you hungry?" He would reply, "Sure Sire! You know everything."

Guru Ji said, "Go, Mardana! Go to the hamlet mentioned as Harrappa, have your meals and return." Mardana said, "No one knows me in town, Sire! Who will give me food without asking for it? If you like, I can go and beg for alms."

Guru Ji: "You, the singer of holy hymns! You do not need to beg. You go to the upper part of the town; there is a home of Khatris; you go and stand there; stay quiet; those people would be having their meals. They would, seeing you, be elated. The entire town would gather there. Hindus and Muslims, all would be falling on your feet, and would present to you a variety of food dishes. Whatever you would taste would be so delicious that you would say in your mind, that you would like to offer your family in exchange. Looking at you, people would be ecstatic and say, O You beautiful creature of the Lord! We are getting thrilled and delighted looking at you.' But Mardana! There would be some people who would not care for you as to who you were and where you had come from."

Listening to this advice, Mardana went to the town, and every word uttered by the complete Guru came out to be true. The entire town came and fell on his feet. A lot of gourmet food, money and clothes were presented; people showered high honors and performed great service. Mardana was thrilled to be so well treated and was unable to contain within himself. Once in a while, someone would show up who would not even look at Mardana. This would dampen his spirits somewhat. This way when the day was over, Mardana collected all the money and clothes in a bundle and brought them to Guru Ji. He looked at Mardana's elation, his mental exuberation and buoyancy, then looked at the silken and cotton clothes and then the money and gold coins. He smiled, and then laughed boisterously looking at all that Mardana had brought. He was rolling on the ground laughing and kept saying, "What have you brought, Mardana?"

Mardana: "True Master! It is all due to the splendor and glory of your words and your Naam. The whole town came to do me many honors; I ate to my fill all the goodies. This money and clothes, I have brought for you."

Guru Ji (pleased): "Mardana! You have done well that you have brought them. Your thought and love is beautiful but these are of absolutely no use to me."

Mardana: "Then what would you like me to do with them?"

Guru Ji: "Throw them away."

Mardana took one look at the cheerful face of Guru Ji, second look within himself, then, again, looked at the lustrous forehead from where a ray of bright light was emanating. Just as the moon sprinkles moonlight, similarly, Guru's face was spreading brilliance all over. Mardana, then picked up the bundle, took it to a distant place and threw it away.

46. SAJJAN THUG (Swindler, Cheat, Trickster)

Guru Ji left this place as well. Kept walking until they reached a development, called Tulambha. They were still some distance away from the town that they saw a big home that happened to be on the roadside. There was a fence around this house. On one side, in the middle, was a door and a portico in front of it. On both sides were religious quarters; on one side a temple for Hindus and on the other, mosque for Muslims. After going through the door, there was an open courtyard and then a large mansion. There were rooms and cellars in the mansions. Behind a camouflage, was hidden a well, passage to whom was secret and was underground. Besides, there were many other courtyards and rooms. The only owner of the mansion and many of his servants and attendants were living there.

The owner's name was Sheikh Sajjan. He had skillfully developed a contrivance of love and service. If a Hindu would come, he would do a great service; would take him to the temple and show him the worship being performed, thus establishing his bona fides as a religious man. If a Muslim traveler would arrive, he would take him to the mosque; would show his hospitality by offering excellent foods and drinks. At night, he would ask them to go to their rooms to rest and sleep. Thus, winning their confidence, he would keep them for a day or two. However, when he got a chance, he would kill them, throw them in the well, and later bury them deep in some unknown place, and would keep all the belongings of the victims. But, during the day, he would display a long rosary to pull the wool over people's eyes. In his mansion, he had made many other arrangements to deceive and rob the travelers.

Guru Ji knew all this. Knowingly, he went to the house of this thug. When Sajjan saw him, he thought "that the Guru was some wealthy person or a jeweler. He has concealed on himself gems and diamonds. The splendor and the brilliance of his face signifies his riches. To disguise all his wealth, he has adopted the guise of an ascetic so that no one could suspect that he was an affluent well-to-do person. Asceticism was a ploy to concoct and conceal his wealth. Therefore, we shall rob them of all the jewels after we send them to sleep." With these thoughts, he was very hospitable to both Mardana and Guru Ji.

Guru Ji kept sitting, in his meditation, until late hours at night. Sajjan came and told him a couple of times, "Please go to your beds; it is getting very late. Beds have been made beautifully for you inside." Guru Ji said, "After rendering one hymn on spiritual meditation, we will go to our rooms to sleep." Sajjan, then said, "Well Sir! If the hymn is in praise of the Lord and His worship, please recite, we, too, would like to hear."

Then Guru Ji signalled Mardana to start playing his violin. Mardana played the violin and Guru Ji recited and rendered a Shabad (hymn) in Raag Soohi Mahalla 1 Ghar 6 when paraphrased was as follows:

> "The white metal is used for making pots and pans. They look polished, but as they are rubbed around, the smudge comes of them. Our friends are those (saints) who will stand by us under all circumstances; whenever and wherever we are asked to explain, they are seen standing there. We keep having expectations from buildings, homes, and mansions inside which pictures have been painted; when they are demolished, they are empty from inside. The white heron clad in white color stands in water with eyes closed pretending to be deeply religious. But by taking advantage of any opportunity, he would eat live fish by diving deep into water. They are not white, meaning they do not deserve to be characterized as saints. People make mistakes looking at me, taking me as a saint, just as a parrot loses its perspective looking at the fake flowers of bombux, a silk tree. (This was a pointer toward Sajjan being a fraud, a cheat and a hypocrite.) The blind man is carrying a lot of load and has to travel a mountainous trek. The path towards the Lord is extremely difficult and steep. We cannot keep track of the trail; how can we complete our journey. Referring to ploys and misdeeds of Sajjan, Guru Ji said no wisdom will be of any avail. Only salvation is through the meditation of Naam which only can break our shackles and redeem us."

As Guru Ji was articulating the hymn he would repeatedly render the central idea, would keep looking towards Sajjan and the meanings of the hymn continued to penetrate into Sajjan's mind. When the hymn and its rendering, that had taken a long time, was over, Sajjan was awakened; all of his frauds and sins and the travelers that he had swindled and killed, started to pass in front of his eyes; he got a sudden twitch inside himself that said to him, "I am ultimately going to die; all this wealth collected through sinful acts would be left for someone else to enjoy but all the nooses would be on my neck in the royal court of law of the Lord. This saint has sung an absolute truth. He felt another twitch that this man is not a jeweler nor has he in his possession gems and diamonds; he is in fact a beloved of the Lord who has rectified all my base acts. Whatever he sang was all about my own transgressions and he has explained them to me so beautifully. The brilliance and splendor that I have seen on his face is the effect of God's worship and meditation." Sajjan got up in a melancholy, rueful and disconsolate mood and fell on Guru's feet and stayed there; kept saying again and again, “O Benefactor! Kindly take mercy on me and grant me forgiveness.”

Guru Nanak Ji, then said, “Sajjan! The sins are forgiven, and kindness, grace and mercy are also showered but under two conditions. One, that you adopt the ‘truth’; truthfully, you must pledge against all your previous sins, frauds and base acts. Secondly, give away all the wealth collected with fraudulent means under the Name of the Lord; give it back to them or their survivors whom you have robbed if you can remember their whereabouts.”

Sajjan solemnly swore with folded hands before Guru Ji and conceded that he was a sinner, that he would not deny, and that he would not commit any of those sins again. He, then, showed the amassed wealth to Guru Ji which at the day break, he started to dispatch to the known addresses, thus giving away all that he had.

After dissipating and distributing the wealth gratis, then Guru Ji also persuaded him to have the mansion, built out of sinned wealth, demolished. Guru Baba ordered, “That, instead, there should be built a religious center, a real place of worship built with honest and pious money where you should meditate, remember His Naam and perform real service to the unfortunate and distressed people.”

Sajjan fell on Guru Ji’s feet. Satguru blessed him with the boon of Naam and made him a holder of Naam. Sajjan spent the rest of his life meditating the Naam, worshipping, doing good deeds, and singing the holy hymns that Mardana had rendered there and preaching them. That was the first religious center that Guru Ji got built.

Sajjan’s mausoleum is still there and is near the Bhai Jodh’s religious center in the Tulambha area.

47. AMELIORATION OF A SAINT (SPIRITUAL GUIDE)

After reforming Sajjan, the thug, into the Sajjan, the saint, Guru Ji moved on. While they were walking, Mardana asked, “Sire! Why did you go to the house of such a ruthless sinner and murderer Sajjan and risk your most precious life?”

Guru Ji: “Mardana! Don’t you think that it is a noble act to convert a dirty pond into a clean and sweet water spring? See! It is not just one who has been delivered but numerous more innocent men have been saved that he was going to kill. Secondly, with his changed disposition, many would learn and become virtuous and charitable in his company, and the poor would be benefacted. With just one reformed person, a sort of stream of goodnesses will start to flow. These swindlers and thugs have some kind of power which because of debased and malicious thoughts gets misdirected, and forces them to commit sins and murders. If they are counseled, and their thoughts set in the right direction, the same power can be harnessed for noble deeds."

Mardana: "I agree, Sire! Truly, these thieves, robbers, plunderers, gamblers and the tyrants have special powers. These fools misuse it in the wrong direction. You have very correctly said that if their eyes can be opened then their internal strength can be channelled towards goodness, virtue and kindness. But my benefactor! You yourself, have enormous powers that you are able to redirect even the powerful ones from evil and wickedness towards virtuosity. Great you are, and great is your Nirankar! Well Sire! Where are we now heading towards? I thought we were going toward Multan but, instead, you have rerouted yourself in the easterly direction."

Sri Guru Ji: "Mardana! We are going towards Nili, the site near the confluence of the rivers Sutlej and Beas. A 'spiritual guide' lives there who is hurting the public."

Mardana: "I hope that the saint we are going to would not be, like Sajjan, after our lives and it will pass comfortably and uneventfully."

Guru Ji: "Do not worry. God will do well."

With such conversation, they kept walking, making stops enroute, for couple of days and nights. Finding a high and a clean spot outside the next village, in a deserted area, they encamped there under a large tree. One of the local villagers happened to pass by. When he saw Guru Nanak, he was greatly pleased. He paid his obeisance, sat there for a little while and then went back to the village. There, he told the people that a beloved of the Lord, with an extremely charming, saintly, chaste and beautiful face was sitting on the ridge outside the village. The village people, thus, came to have a glimpse of him. Everyone who saw him was simply thrilled. Many of them asked him to move into the village, and stay in a beautiful and comfortable home. But Guru Ji declined. He remained there for a few days. In the meantime, the Pir—the spiritual guide, about whom he had made reference to Mardana earlier, came to know that some saint had landed on the high hill, who was charming and elegant, imbued in Lord's love, and had absolutely no greed or avarice. His music was enticing. A little later, someone came and told him again, "The newly arrived saint is going to build his abbey on the top of the hill, will also make a few rooms as well." Hearing this, the Pir was angered.

This saint had toiled considerably, and used to do penance and religious austerity not to inculcate the love of God, but to win the appreciation and praise of the people that he was great and with miraculous powers. People were afraid of him and were, out of stark fear, worshipping him. If someone would not accept his authority, he would get mad. This way, he had created some sort of awesome terror about himself. He used to live on a second story flat and would not allow anyone else to build a second story in their homes.

Guru Nanak Dev Ji did not appreciate this type of attitude. His point was that a person who claims to be a saint, or a spiritual guide, should be enamored with the love of God; he should not have any kind of greed for money, materials or wealth; he should work for the good of the public, help the needy and the afflicted and put them in touch with the devotion of the Lord, thus making them happy and comfortable. That is why, Guru Ji went there. If he were able to change him into a real truthful, honest and pious saint, then all those people, who owe allegiance to him, would be greatly benefitted.

When the Pir (a Muslim saint) got the news that another godly person had arrived and people had started regarding him superior, he became jealous and anxious lest someone claiming and proving to be more exalted than him might not undermine his grandeur and praise. Then someone also told him that the new saint (Guru Ji) was planning to build a home on the high ridge and would put the second story as well. He was further burnt and agitated. The fact was that the Pir himself used to live on a second floor room, and if anyone dared to build the second story of his home, the Pir would have it razed. At that time, it was the reign of Muslims, and no Muslim would put a check on any of his excesses. If he were to indulge in any other kind of oppression or outrage against Hindu masses, no ruler would stop him. That was another reason of official abetment, that people were mighty afraid of him.

When he heard talks about Guru Ji, he was further infuriated and decided to go to him and push him away from the area. "No one would be allowed in my village with a second story to his house," he said.

So, after paying his courtesies, he sat in front of Guru Ji. He thought in his mind that the new saint was a Hindu, and that the Pir would be able to win over him in a matter of a short discussion of a few moments. Then asked, "O Saint! Where have you come from and where are you heading to?"

Guru Ji: "The wind blows from one side and goes through the other. Wind is always on a move, and we say that it is coming and going."

Pir: "I understand that you will stay here. If you do, would you like us to build a house for you so that you can do your prayers and meditation steadily here?"

Guru Ji: "We are not becoming static yet. We have a command to keep moving from place to place."

Pir: (A little relieved) "I had heard that you will build a 2-storied house."

Guru Ji: "Will we build or demolish? The home of a saint is the upper story of the Lord."

Pir: "I didn't understand the 'building and demolishing' part."

Guru Ji: "It is said (and I am sure, you know it) that a man is made out of earth; he is deeply in love with himself; one, he has a body out of earth, and second, he, building a house from earth, occupies it with arrogance that he owns it. But as soon as he receives a message from the Lord, leaving both the mud structures (his body and home) here, he departs. To get stuck in mud is to have mud-like unclean intellect. The saints are supposed to be of sparkling clean and radiant intellect. He, divorcing himself away from the mud, looks at it, and says that it is not me nor for me. The God's spiritual chamber is above the mud structure and the saint, going into that higher chamber, resides there. Getting up, sitting down, walking around or sleeping, he stays with the Lord. The saint operates and plays in that high chamber. The love for mud takes us toward mud and the mud chambers, with the passage of time, become graveyards, tombs and cremation grounds."

This advice of Guru Ji is extremely valuable. Its simple meanings are: "O saint! Your body is made out of mud i.e., it is made of five elements like wind, water, fire, mud and sky. You have a spirit inside you; that is life. It is therefore desirable that you love your life and lift yourself up to a high idealed life; the wise say that you become a 'pure spirit'. You have been going towards losses when you started loving the mud-brick structures. You have such an obsession with them that you started to torment others. When you demolish someone's second story, they are pained and they cry. You had become a Pir, a Pir is supposed to be great, and the great are supposed to comfort the lowly ones."

"Therefore sir! the intense love for the second story structure became so painful. Anything that gives pain is lowly. Do you realize that, ultimately, after death, you will be buried in a grave in the earth and your body, leaving the second story chamber, would not stay on the earth and rather go even lower below the earth in an excavated spot. Your bewitchment for higher chamber of mud and brick, would keep your life, spirit and mind, all in a grave. What was required, on the other hand, was that after your death, your soul/life should have reached the Waheguru, and only the body should have been buried below the ground." This was the explanation of Guru Ji's sermon, and the saint understood it well.

Hearing the truthful and sanctimonious discourse of Guru Ji, the Pir was awakened and came to his senses, and immediately realized that he had been involved in sins and maliciously low actions. Then, with folded hands, he beseeched Guru Ji to extend his stay there for a few more days. Guru Ji agreed to stay on a little longer. The Pir, enjoying the noble company of Guru Ji everyday, in fact, became a true saint and began silent repetitions and meditation of His Naam. It dawned on him clearly that all men were the creations of the Lord, all were His children. We should love them all and torment none. One, he became conscious of the deep devotion for Waheguru, and secondly, he was also blessed with the boon that we should always live under and accept His Will. This way, making the Pir chaste and pious for himself and responsible for spreading love for humanity amongst the people, Guru Ji moved on. Just as, Guru Ji, by reforming a thug into a noble person had enhanced the spiritual welfare of the world, similarly, he was instrumental to set a misdirected Pir on the right track to add to the overall comfort of the world. By reshaping one by one, he was able to make thousands of people more at ease and happy. We should therefor repeat:

> "Great is Guru Nanak, Great is Guru Nanak
> Great is Sri Guru Nanak Dev Ji."

48. TRIP TO HARIDWAR

Remaining with Pir for a few days and realizing that he had really transformed him, and had started him moving on the right track, Guru Ji took leave of him, and set out in the easterly direction. He stopped at several places; gave life-saving advice to the people and directed them towards the path of goodness, godliness and benevolence. Walking for several days, Guru Ji, finally, reached Haridwar. It has not been well ascertained so far as to which places he stopped and what kind of wonders he performed on the way but fragrance, wherever it goes, shall spread fragrance. It is, therefore, not difficult to understand that he kept emancipating people all over and all through wherever he went.

Haridwar is a town on the banks of river Ganges (Ganga) about where the river flows leaving the mountains and coming into the plains. This place is a pilgrimage center and has been considered a holy spot from olden times. People from all across India come here, take their dip in Ganges and consider that all of their sins have been washed away. Here on the bank of Ganges, too, Guru Ji came to put the people living there as well as the pilgrims on the correct path.

One day, early in the morning, he went to Brahm Kund (tank) where Brahma, the Lord, was supposed to have taken a bath, and stood there. He saw many people bathing there and they were throwing handfuls of water towards the rising sun in the east. The charming Guru Ji also went to stand in the waters of Ganges. He kept his back towards the sun and contrary to the practice of the people, started throwing handfuls of water towards the west. It was something completely new. People watching it gathered there. When it became a sizable crowd, they asked him, "Who are you and why are you throwing water in the westerly direction? In the westerly direction is the Mecca. Tell us, are you a Hindu or a Muslim? You seem to be a Hindu, and should be throwing water in the easterly direction towards the sun."

Guru Ji looked at them mercifully and compassionately, and asked, "Why do you throw water towards the east?" They replied, "We are sending water to our ancestors," and some said, "we are sending water to the sun." Guru Ji, then, asked, "How far is the abode of your ancestors?" They answered, "Forty nine and half millions of miles away are our ancestors and so is the sun millions and millions of miles."

On this, Guru Ji, again, started splashing additional waters towards the west. People asked him, again, "Well! Give us an answer, whom are you sending the waters to?"

Satguru replied, "Listen friends! My village lies in this direction. I have my field there. There has not been any rains in our area. I, watching you all, am sending my water to my arid fields. If it reaches there, it can save my crops." People started laughing and one of them said, "Your water, taken from Ganges is falling into Ganges itself. How do you think it will reach your fields?"

Guru Ji: "O.K. brother! I agree that my water cannot reach my fields which are about two hundred and fifty miles only but please tell me, how would your water reach millions of miles from here?"

Every little action of the Sri Guru Ji had a great significance. He said the above short sentence casually, but it sent all those present in deeper thoughts, that "if throwing water the way we are throwing cannot reach on this earth itself, how could it reach millions and millions of miles out towards the sun or the ancestors? He seems to be speaking the truth. He is some angel who has come to render advice to us." But someone also from the crowd said, "My good man! It is a matter of resolve. Our mental resolves are offering the waters."

Guru Ji said, "I have the resolve of Hari, Hari in my mind. Your resolves have gone home; some towards your sons, some towards your wives, your wealth, shops and businesses, some towards your friends and others towards the enemies. So your mind is focused on other things. You keep repeating orally the words, Hari, Hari but your mind's resolves are not for Hari (the Lord)."

Then a man asked the Guru, "Where do you think the resolves of my mind is?"

Guru Ji: "Your mind, while turning the beads of your rosary, had gone to your wife." Similarly, Guru Ji told the mental notions of a few others which turned out to be true. Now, the people were convinced and fell at his feet.

A large crowd had gathered at the steps of the banks of Ganges. When Guru Baba saw that all those people were willing to listen to the truth, he thunderously sermonized there and told them the right way to truth. Then, he taught them the manner of developing devotion for Waheguru, to do good deeds for others and not to hurt anyone. He advised them "lift your minds by residing the Lord inside you, become benefactors, give charities, stay tranquil and distribute tranquility, and eat/drink the food earned out of an honest living whether you are in service, business, farming or labor; put in hand work with truthfulness and piety and do not let any sins or misdeeds enter your *modus operandi.* Waheguru is inside everyone and, therefore, consider everyone a brother, a part of a larger family; Waheguru is always with us; keep this awe and fear before you; do not commit any sins because He does not like sins at all. Waheguru is love, and you should love Him."

When Guru Ji had finished such a long sermon, people said, "Sir! Food is ready. Let us go to eat." Guru Ji was a little hesitant, but the people persisted, "For God's sake! Please join us." Guru Ji, then went along with those people to eat. When he reached the kitchen, many well known and big priests and saints entered the kitchen and drew lines.

Guru Ji asked, "Brothers! Is the kitchen defiled, why are you drawing these lines?" They replied, "We have had the food prepared under our direct supervision; we didn't let the kitchen to be desecrated, and the lines have been drawn so that no one should come into the kitchen from the front side."

The Guru Baba said, "So long as you were not in the kitchen, it was a pious place. Now that you have come here, it has been contaminated because a few of the low caste persons have also come in."

They said, "Guru Ji! We are unable to see them."

Guru Ji: "People consider the following four castes as low: Bards, butchers, sweepers, and merciless wicked persons (who remove the hides of animals). I consider the following characteristics as four low castes: Evil thoughts, lack of compassion, slander (evil speaking or vituperation) of others and anger." After recounting these, Guru Ji then addressed himself to those priests and saints who had drawn the lines, and who considered themselves truthful and pious, "When you entered the kitchen, you had these lowly inferior characteristics in you, therefore, you were defiled and thus belonged to the low castes. The good characteristics lead to good actions and soiled characteristics to sins and misdeeds." The Guru Baba, thus, drove home good advice so that they were able to drive out all old bad habits. Keeping the old base habits would have made it extremely difficult, if not impossible, for them to become pure, solemn, or holy.

Those, who had come along, and who had invited him for food, started thinking that Guru Baba had said the truth. One of them, then asked with folded hands, "How do we become holy?"

Guru Ji rendered a hymn at that time which meant: Adopt the truth, be truthful; instead of drawing lines in the kitchen to maintain its sacrosanct, or making trips again and again roaming at holy places and taking baths there, you should remember Lord's Naam. This is truthful and chaste bath. Similarly, stay away from other types of sins; never commit any misdeeds. Its results would be, that in the land of Waheguru, you would be considered superior. You would go there as a clean, pure, beautiful and a good person.

Hearing this, they all fell at his feet and said, "Kindly adopt us as your own." Guru Ji then said, "All the wealth you have amassed by cheating and defrauding the public should be given away." At this, whatever they had with them like money, gold coins, goods and other wealth such as horses, chariots, was collected from their camps, brought up and given away to the poor and the needy. Guru Ji became merciful on them. The Master of the world, Guru Nanak, gave them the sermon of Naam. He dyed their hearts with a thick and lasting coat of Naam. He gave coolness to their burning minds; it made them comfortable. When their time of death came, they were redeemed from transmigration. They had maintained a constant and deep devotion to Naam with their mind and soul during their life times.

49. TRIP TO KURUKSHETRA

Guru Ji, again, moved, and this time in the north westerly direction towards the town of Saharan Pur. There was a fair being held on the way but Guru Ji kept walking and reached Kurukshetra. Stopping at several places on the way, he spread the sermon of Satnam; reformed the actions of the people, and taught them to do good deeds and stay away from misdeeds and sins.

A large fair was being held in Kurukshetra at that time. Hundreds of thousands of men, women and children, from far and near, used to gather there, and did so even on that day. It was the occasion of solar eclipse. People were coming together to take their baths. Guru Ji had gone there neither to see the fair, nor to become chaste and holy by taking a dip. He was holy and chaste from the very beginning. He had gone there to bring good sense to the lost and misdirected people.

Common people believed that when the lunar or solar eclipse took place, two demons, named, Rahu and Ketu circumscribed the moon and sun extremely tightly with the intent of killing them. That is why, people took baths and gave alms so that with bathing and charities, the demons might flinch away and might not be able to exercise their evil effects. This belief was not correct because the eclipse was only an image (shadow) sometimes, of earth and sometimes of moon, on moon and the sun. We can well appreciate that if someone kept a record of all eclipses of seventeen years every year, then all the future eclipses of the next 17 years could be forecasted because after certain time periods, the eclipses do take place (almost) around the same dates. It has been determined that according to the set movements of the earth and the moon, their shadows are cast at different times. So, Guru Ji, went there to eradicate the fantasy and the misbelief about demons and to spread the true enlightenment and knowledge of the Creator that you may, ordinarily, give charities, take a bath everyday but do not get frightened and/or get terrorized by the non-existing demons or with false beliefs. Satguru Ji, again, went to give another advice that the creator of the entire universe was the Lord Himself. How did he create? This is known only to Him, "Therefore, moon, sun, stars, earth, human beings, and animals are all His creations; do not forget Him; remember Him, love Him and do only those deeds that are agreeable to Him; and considering the deeds that are not agreeable with Him as 'undesirable', abstain from them. Eliminate all kinds of suspicions and superstitions."

His purpose to go to the crowds of Kurukshetra was to dispel the darkness (ignorance) and to preach the love of Waheguru. He used to teach his disciples (Sikhs) that all creations belong to Him. "When you remember the Lord, you love Him, then do not impose any kind of sufferings or pains on His originations; do not cheat, deceive and defraud anyone, operate truthfully and love everyone."

50. ECLIPSE

Just about at the time of eclipse, Raja Jagat Rai, son of Raja Amrit Rai of Hansi arrived in Kurukshetra, accompanied by his mother (the queen mother). He had been deposed by his opponents and expelled. The purpose of his visit to Kurukshetra was to meet some saint(s) and seek his blessings so that he could get his rule back. It seemed that he knew about the huge fair being held there, but was not aware that the eclipse was to be the same day, the day of his arrival. On the way, he went hunting and shot a deer so that after encamping, and having his meals, he would, then, meet saints and ascetics. But he found Guru Ji sitting a distance before the pilgrimage centers. Mardana was singing holy hymns (Kirtans). Seeing the divine face, both Raja (Prince) and his mother were simply amazed lest he was the true and real beloved of the Lord. They stepped forward, bowed before Guru Ji and presented the deer to him. Raja, then, explained his horror story. With his order, the deer was put in a pot to cook. Guru Ji kept listening to his sorrows, kept encouraging him and imparting enlightenment. In the meantime, seeing a stack of smoke going up into the air, people became agitated because it was considered a sin to cook anything during the eclipse. Therefore, the crowd, with sticks and clubs in their hands angered over this transgression came and shouted in their wrath, "Who are you to cook food at the eclipse time, and more so who are you to kill a deer and then cook it?"

Guru Ji spoke: "Welcome friends! You can very well kill us, but just think that if cooking of a deer in a pot during the time of eclipse is a sin, how would the killing of all of us make you benefactors? If you think that it would be a good deed, please go ahead and do it." Everyone started pondering over his remarks. It appeared that on the one hand, Guru Ji accepted defeat that, 'come and kill me,' but on the other, it turned out to be a victory. All of them were ashamed of their irrationality and they put down all the clubs and sticks. Guru Ji told them, "If you want to discuss or exchange thoughts, please bring some pundits or saints, and I will be more than willing to meet with them." They all went and brought with them a few learned (pundit) and saintly persons. The name of one of them was 'Nanu' but he called himself, 'Nanak'. He had studied, researched and understood the scriptures that it was time for Nanak, a beloved incarnation of the Lord to appear. He claimed that he was a learned and a great sage and he would be able to steer the mission of meditation. He changed his name from Nanu to Nanak so that he can become a famous prophet. He was one of the group of Pundits who had just arrived. He kept wondering, from where could another Nanak appear in the fair? Could he be the same, about whom, he had read so much in the scriptures? He was a well read person and was confident to win him over with a discussion. That was the reason, he had joined the bunch of mendicants and ascetics who had come to exchange ideas. He opened up the discussion, "In our Shastras (scriptures), meat is forbidden. Our ancestors, from the olden times of Vedas (scriptures) have remained non-violent and did not eat animal flesh. You being a Hindu, why are you going contrary to the Shastras?"

Guru Ji said, "Brother! If you were of another religion, it would have been different. But O Nanu! You talk of Vedas, Puranas, other Shastras (scriptures) and of ancestors. Listen and think! Your ancestors used to organize big feasts; they would kill horses, rhinoceroses and other animals, put them in the fire worships as religious sacrifices, and would offer them as oblations to the gods and goddesses. You have meat in your Puranas, and Ramayan. At the time of weddings, you kill goats and cook them and claim to be Khatris. The Aryans used to kill animals and ate their meat. How can you say that in your religion and in the scriptures, meat is forbidden?"

"Again, Pundit Ji! The Khatris, who are your hosts, have been eating meat. You receive charities from them. Can you remain religious by accepting alms from meat eaters? Is there not a touch of violence in the charity of the giver?"

"Pandit Ji! The fact of the matter is that many amongst you have become slick and skillful talkers. They are not living holy lives; are not men of compassion, love, real knowledge and concentration. They make up a few expressions and quarreling and contending, try to have a victory over the majority of the Brahmins-the learned ones. They consider it superiority. But this is mere cunningness or tactfulness. Anyone whose mental eyes have not been opened up, who have not realized the true knowledge about and felt the all-powerful Waheguru, and those who do not develop within them the humility, mercy and compassion when they look at other human beings, you may call them superior, learned, devotees, or lovers of the Creator, but they are none of these. One Pundit says, you can eat meat, the other says; you can't. Then both the Pundits start altercating and disputing; this is called 'squabbling'. The squabbles last for days; people watch the fun of one winning and the other losing. Both are high in their ego and haughtiness. The winner gloats and shows arrogance of his victory and the other sobs, cries and is ashamed in the agony of defeat. Neither one has enlightenment, knowledge, meditation or devotion. That is the reason that you have not been able to do good for the world, at large. You are simply showing self conceit."

Guru Ji made several more similar remarks. The listeners and the audience were all greatly impressed and bowed in reverence. Nanu held Guru's feet, and, with folded hands, accepted his omissions and commissions of deliberately changing his name to Nanak from Nanu, just to win cheap popularity. He said, "I wasn't aware that you were here. I was, even after all the studies and research, still uneducated, uninformed and ignorant; in addition, I was haughty, egotistic and greedy, too. You are the real incarnation and you are, truly, the Nanak. [The word 'Nanak' means an embodiment of eternal elation, ease, goodness and comfort.] You are the emancipator of Kalyug! You are the one to grant salvation to all! I will, from today, call myself Nanu and not Nanak." He then addressed the audience, "People! The real 'Nanak' has come. I am not Nanak." At that time, all Pundits, scholars and ascetics gathered there, paid their respects by bowing before Guru Ji with humility. Many adopted his followship (Sikhism) and received the blessings of Naam. (The place where this discussion took place, is still there in Kurukshetra and a Gurdwara stands there.)

51. CONCLUSION

In this episode, Sri Guru Nanak Sahib, first some of them, and then all those who came later, through exchange of ideas and discussions, made them completely helpless; they became utterly unresponsive. It was something like this: Assume that a master is taking a bundle of wood laden on the back of a camel. On the way, if the camel became resistive and refused to move, then if the master, taking one of the sticks from the laden wood uses the same stick to make the camel move, similarly, Sri Guru Nanak Dev Ji, gave an argument to those who came to kill him that if the killing of a deer by the prince during the time of eclipse was a misdeed and a sin, then, how would your action to kill me during the eclipse time be otherwise? See that Guru Ji belied them on their own turf and they were chagrined.

Same way, when the Pundits and ascetics said that meat was forbidden in Hindu religion, Guru Ji argued with them based on the old scriptures, that their ancestors used to kill all kinds of animals, put them in the fire worships and offered them as oblations, they would try to transmit meat to the gods and goddesses; how can you assert that meat was a taboo in Hindu religion, Shastras, Puranas and in the actions of your forefathers? The visitors were all embarrassed and stopped quibbling about this. Guru Ji, also, advised them, "You should not start controversies and arguments on every little silly issue; rather spend your time in loving Waheguru, remembering His Naam and remain within His knowledge and concentration. Where you should develop a deep devotion with the Creator, you should not hurt or torment His creations. Be good to them because they are all His children. You should love the entire world the same way."

Regarding meals, Guru Ji gave the following advice:

> Baba (Nanak) says food and pleasure are obloquy and infancy
> If they manifest pain in the bodies and immortal deeds in the mind.

This command of Guru Sahib is still aptly applicable to every place of every country. "Do not eat any such food that can result in some form of discomfort leading to different kinds of ailments in your body; do not consume any such food that might be responsible for the creation of immoral manifestation in the mind. e.g., eating too many peppers and chilies can make you irritable and angry; eating too much fats can make you inert and lethargic, and, perhaps, towards high cholesterol, leading to heart attack; and similar other things that can cause to form evil ideas inside us should be avoided. Everyone should decide for himself at any given situation." This is a Shastra of eating and drinking given by Sri Guru Nanak Sahib Ji that is usefully applicable in all circumstances.

Another miracle of Guru Ji of that time is also mentioned in the history books. When all those present were impressed with the sound advice of Guru Sahib, and became his adherents, he ordered to open the pot full of meat that had already been cooked up to eat. When the pot was opened, to the utter amazement of all, it was full of rice pudding (khir). That was distributed to Pundits and other common people as a 'blessed food'. They all ate it and were convinced:

"Guru Nanak has come to grant salvation in Kalyug."

52. MANSUKH—SHIVNABH

Sri Guru Nanak Dev Ji, leaving his household, business and shop, and everything else behind, keeping the service of Waheguru as foremost, trekked his way to Haridwar; from there, he walked to Kurukshetra at the happening of 'eclipse episode,' already described above. On the other side, his devoted disciple, Mansukh, who used to live in Lahore doing his business there, travelled all the way from his home to Sangladeep, an island on the southern tip of India, today known as Sri Lanka, on a business trip. There, a certain day was scheduled to be a day of fasting during which no food except only a little bit of fruit was to be eaten. This practice of fasting was considered a virtue, a noble act. Everyone went on fast but Mansukh didn't.

By not following them, people became displeased with Mansukh, and the officials of the ruler (Raja) came, arrested him and took him before the Raja. The Raja asked, "O stranger! You appear to be a Hindu. Why didn't you keep the fast? Why didn't you participate in the worship and the bath?"

Mansukh: "O Raja! I am an aspirant to meet the Lord-Parmeshwar. There are two ways to reach Him; one is to go there extremely slowly by crawling like an ant, and the other is to fly like a bird. I am one who follows the path of the bird. Fasts, other practices, rites and rituals such as bathing at holy places, etc. are like an 'ant path' which are very, very gradual in nature. My path is to fly like a bird and reach my destination fast."

Raja was surprised and asked, "Would you please tell us about that path?"

Mansukh: "Raja! That route is to love the Parmeshwar-the Creator; remembering him in the heart all the times and realizing that He is inside, and is always near. I keep remembering Him, I love Him, and adore Him internally. Whomsoever we remember constantly and devotedly in our hearts, we become closer to him. Worshipping, reciting His Naam, penance, hard meditation, wandering at the holy places of pilgrimage are all actions that generate vanity and ego; that I am superior, I am a meditator, I keep fasts. We keep repeating I, I, me, me - this is self conceit. We show off and pose to be stiff necked amongst people. By so doing, we are creating a distance between Waheguru and ourselves. We get so much wrapped around ourselves and do not get to pay attention towards Him. But if you keep the Creator within you and love Him, self ego in minimized. Just as a mother loves her child, a son loves his father, the person loving forgets his/her own pleasures and comforts for those of the beloved. Is it true or not? The mother will provide food to child even at the cost of remaining hungry."

Raja: "O trader! Where have you learnt about this flying path?"

Mansukh: "From my true Guru (teacher)."

Raja: "Who is such a teacher?"

Mansukh: "Raja Ji! Please listen! That teacher has landed from the land of Waheguru to grant emancipation and salvation in Kalyug. He is always in constant touch with Waheguru, and endeavors to connect others as well to Him. He is the epitome and an embodiment of love. A glimpse of him would automatically attract you towards him."

Raja: "What is his name?"

Mansukh's eyes looked up, got filled with emotional tears of love and devotion, and said with a minor quiver in his body:

> "Sri Guru Nanak Dev
> Sri Guru Nanak Dev
> Who has come to redeem the Kalyug."

It is not known with what kind of love, emotional buoyancy, or deep affection had Mansukh called out Guru Ji's name, but immediately after the Raja heard Guru Ji's name, an unusual shivering ran through his body. His eyes got filled with devotional tears and it appeared that he, too, had fallen in deep love and affection with Guru Ji, and he became extremely anxious and developed a yearning to meet him as soon as possible. After quite a while, the Raja said, "Mansukh! Take me with you, get me a glimpse of Him and let me meet the beloved Guru. This rule, reign and resources and good fortune are nothing. Get me divorced from them all and take me to him." Then Mansukh said, "Raja! There is no need to give up your royal posture, your territory or your rule. Sitting here, you can rule justly and honestly! but remember Guru Nanak, the charming Guru Nanak, in your heart with utmost devotion. Consider him your own, consider him near you. Pulled by the force of your love, he will come here to give you a glimpse of himself, caress you and grant you redemption from transmigration."

Raja developed an affinity for Mansukh. He would invite him every day, listen about the virtues of Guru Ji, and would have increasing desire, eagerness and enthusiasm to meet him. Just as, Mansukh was enamored with Guru Ji, similar bewitchment was also developed within the Raja for Guru Ji. Mansukh assured him that the Guru would go wherever there was affection and dedication and would provide an opportunity to touch his feet.

Arousing a strong yearning, and detailing a description of the symptoms and signs of the Guru, Mansukh returned from Sangladeep to his home.

53. PANI PAT

Guru Ji, leaving Kurukshetra, started walking towards the southwest and arrived at Pani Pat, a town on the road to Delhi, and sat down, outside the town, near a well.

In the meantime, a disciple of some other saint came there. His real name was Sheikh Tahar, but people called him Sheikh Tatihari. When he looked towards the well, he seemed to realize that a Muslim Pir or a saint was sitting there. He addressed Guru Ji, "O, saint of Allah! Respects-salutations to you - Salam - U - Lekam (a Muslim way of greetings)." But Guru Ji did not respond like a Muslim would, namely, "Wa Alekam Salam, respects and salutations to you too." Rather he said, "You disciple of your Pir! We salute the Creator." Tatihari was astonished, and told his mentor, on return, "I have today met a mendicant - saint who has turned the salutations around and said something strange and unusual, namely, 'Salutations to the Lord'." The Pir said, "If he was saluting the Allah, he must be an elderly great saint. Let us go, I want to get a glimpse of him." Both of them arrived at the well. The Pir who was known by the name 'Sharaf' greeted him by saying 'Salam-U-Lekam'. The Guru replied the same way as before, 'Salam to the Lord'. Pir, then, asked him, "You do not have any bag or baggage, you look like a saint, would you please answer questions if I were to ask some?" Guru Ji said, "Sure".

Pir asked many questions to which Guru Ji gave apt answers. The crux of Guru Ji's replies was something like this: "A saint, an ascetic, a mendicant or a beloved of the Lord is someone who dies living, i.e., he does not commit any base acts, does not hurt anyone, does not overlook the Lord even for a moment, does not get angry, does claim only his own right and share, does not usurp other's rights, isn't greedy, does remember and meditate His Naam daily, and sitting in solitude, concentrates his attention and mind towards Him. Such a person may be called a real and true saint, an ascetic, a mendicant or a Muslim Pir."

Sheikh Sharaf, then said, "Wonderful, wonderful, you are indeed a man of God. He, who has recognized Him, does not need to be asked or tested more. A glimpse of him is sufficient." He came forward, shook Guru's hands, then kissed his feet, and, later, returned to his abode.

After this, Guru Ji and Mardana moved on.

54. DELHI

Guru Ji left Pani Pat, and making stops and emancipating people on the way reached Delhi, and encamped a couple of miles before Delhi on the banks of river, Jamuna. A saint named, Majnu, used to live there. Nearby was a stable for elephants of the then ruler Ibrahim Lodhi. The portion of the town where Guru Ji was sitting, was called Timar Pur and the village nearby, Chandrawal. Guru Ji lodged himself under the trees on a spot on the bank of Jamuna that was on a much higher level than the river. He spent the night in the love and devotion of Waheguru. In the wee hours of the morning, Mardana completed the Shabad Kirtan (singing of holy hymns), when Guru Ji heard someone crying. Guru Ji sent Mardana to find out who was crying in the early hours, the sublimal time meant to be used to remember and meditate His Naam, and why? Mardana came back after ascertaining and said, "Sire! An elephant has died in the stable and its trainer and his family are crying." The soft hearted and compassionate Guru Ji got up and went to the said spot, and asked them, "Brother! Why are you all crying?"

Trainer: "You blessed soul! Our elephant has died."

Sri Guru Ji: "The elephant belonged to the emperor and he does not care about money. If one elephant is dead, he can and, perhaps, will buy ten more. Why should you cry?"

Trainer: "Sire! We are crying lest we are held responsible for its death and become the targets of the emperor's wrath, that the elephant died due to our negligence. Secondly, we had a modest source of living; he would fire us and we would become unemployed today. When another elephant arrives, who knows whether we would be rehired or not, or our place may be given (or taken) by someone else. It is difficult to find this kind of work. Elephants are not kept by common people; princes and emperors alone can afford them, and it is pretty difficult to secure employment with them." Saying this, they started to cry more loudly.

Guru Ji, compassionate as he was, felt mercy for them and said, "Go and caress its face with your hand and utter the word Waheguru, Waheguru'." On this advice, the trainer went forward, moved his hand back and forth on the face of the elephant and repeated the words, Waheguru, Waheguru, and the elephant began to move and then stood up.

This news reached the emperor of Delhi, Ibraham Lodhi that a saint had arrived in Timarpur, who had revived the royal dead elephant. The emperor sent for the elephant, rode on it and came to see Guru Ji. He got down from the elephant, greeting the Guru sat near him and said, "O saint! Did you revive this elephant?"

Guru Ji replied, "Only God can kill and only He can revive. He alone giveth and taketh life. God becomes merciful in the prayers of saints." The emperor, then, asked him to put the elephant to sleep, namely, to kill it."

Guru Baba, then recited a couplet which meant, "Only He kills and only He brings back, Nanak says, without Him, the One and only One, there is no one else" and the elephant died. The emperor, then, insisted, that Guru Ji revive him back. Guru Ji replied, "Sir! The iron rod

(God) can become red hot in the fire (saint), but if there is no fire at all (as desired by the saints), the iron rod cannot become hot. Similarly if God kills someone, and if a saint prays, the dead can be revived; but if the saint kills someone, he may not get up because God would not alter the deeds of His saints He loves so dearly."

The emperor was greatly pleased hearing and understanding this simile and said, "Kindly accept some monetary or other donation." Guru Ji recited another hymn which meant something like the following:

"I am only hungry for the Lord, and do not care for any money or material things. The only yearning and demand I have is to get one glimpse of Him and nothing else."

55. SHEIKH BAJEED

From Delhi, Guru Ji did not return home, rather moved on. Mardana was with him. He left in the easterly direction. After some distance, he sat down under a tree. Mardana performed the Kirtan and after he had concluded, a saint was seen coming in their direction being carried in a palanquin, being carried by six scullions-servants, who generally, were water carriers, or pot cleaners. It was comfortable for a ride. A little distance where Guru Ji was sitting was a tree with a dense shade. The palanquin bearers put the palanquin down under this tree. Then those servants started to massage the saint who was, by now, lying on a temporary bed made by the servants. One of them was fanning him too. This ascetic was known as Sheikh Bajeed.

This was an unusual sight for Mardana. He asked Guru Ji, "What kind of theatric is this? On the one hand, this saint has been riding a palanquin and on the other, he is tired. He didn't walk even a step. He rode the palanquin all the way. How could he get tired riding and the scullions who carried him all along who should have been tired, are pressing, massaging and fanning him?"

Guru Ji: "Mardana! Those who walk are, generally, stronger. They get a better appetite. Whatever they eat is easily digested, and they remain healthy. They would lose appetite if they would keep sitting; if they ate too much, they would get sick; if they were to eat little, they would lose strength and their bodies get tired fast. Haven't you learnt, 'No one dies of being active; it is the immobility that can kill faster.'"

Mardana: "Sire! But this saint is not old, does not seem to be sick. He appears to be healthy. Why should he get tired?"

Guru Ji smiled and said, "He has two types of fatigues, one from penance and hard meditation from his previous life, the main purpose for which was that he acquired special powers so that people became afraid of him. Secondly, in this life he has become famous; people worship him, give him wealth and materials, and he has become rich. Therefore, now fulfilling peoples' hopes, and living an affluent life in comfort, he has become 'Sitting Mal', an inert person. He gets tired from all this. If he doesn't get pressed, massaged and caressed, how can he get rid of his exhaustion and stay healthy?" Saying this, Guru Ji laughed, again.

What Guru Ji meant was "that we do penance and hard meditation so as to become saints and Pirs; then as saints/Pirs we develop stark ego, start collecting material assets and amass wealth. With this, develops laziness, inertness, letharginess and wretchedness. What ought to be done is that they should love their Waheguru, do good deeds and do no harm to anyone. With this, their bodies and souls will remain oblated and healthy. When they depart from this world, they will go to the land of Waheguru. They, generally end up going to places, where they receive some sort of affection. If they love Waheguru, they will automatically go to His land, but if they love materials, money, spiritual and miraculous powers only, they will not be going to His land. They would continue to wander in the cycles of transmigration hankering after wealth and people's followship.

56. NANAK MATA

Moving around, Guru Ji reached a spot, then known as Gorakh Mata. The forests were nearby. There were abbeys of ascetics of Gorakh religious sect.

Guru Ji sat under a dried (dead) fig tree. A little distance away were smoldering piles of chaff, burning fire, and preparations were underway to prepare food. Mardana went to those ascetics and asked if he could borrow some fire from them. No one obliged him; rather, some of them rebuked and chided him away. Mardana returned disappointed. Guru Ji cajoled, consoled and advised him, "Do not get dejected or saddened; do not get angry. This way, we are apt to forget Waheguru and get mentally hurt. Whatever is done is well done. You come and sit down here holding true faith with Waheguru; He, himself, will worry about us."

On Guru Ji's assurance, Mardana slightly comforted, sat there along with Guru Ji, and soon after fell asleep. In the meantime, a person carrying a load of woods to sell passed by. It was getting dark now and was getting a little cool as well. The man with the woods suddenly became enamored. He prepared a nice fire in front of Guru Ji and Mardana, with his woods. When Mardana got up and was surprised to see Guru Ji's words having come true, again. He began singing the religious hymns, while the fire kept burning.

Guru Ji stayed there for a few days. Leafbuds had started to come out of the dead tree under which he had encamped. The Sidhs (Goraks's followers) realized that he was not an ordinary saint. He was some virtuous person with powers and miracles. Sidhs thought that it would be to their advantage if they can bring him to their fold and make him a Jogi, an ascetic. Then two or three of their leaders came to meet with him respectfully and asked, "Whose disciple are you? From whom have you taken Gurmantra-incantation?" The answer that Guru Ji gave was in the form of Shabad recited in Raag Soohi Mahalla 7 that can be paraphrased as follows:

> "Waheguru is considered so big that He is limitless, and His bounds cannot be perceived. He is the creator. I should always keep Him, my husband, the lover, the beloved, in my mind. I should keep my mind attuned in His meditation. Waheguru has been described as heart rendering, heart comforting and someone who brings general welfare. It is prayed, 'O, Lord! Kindly keep me involved in your love, dedication, and devotion? Being such a great, truthful, pious, and chaste soul himself, Guru Ji shows an utmost humility; he further supplicates that he is blessed with his intellect, wisdom, his tasks, his chores, and his remembrance. 'Considering me as inane, kindly cleanse my thinking process.'"

When the Sidhs heard this hymn, they realized that Guru Ji was godly, and a complete person, i.e., he was a beloved of the Lord, and was apt in his dedication for Waheguru. They should not enter into any conflict with him. Rather, they should try to make him their follower. If he could adopt their cult, and become a Jogi, it would be a definite advantage and a positive addition to their sect. They said, "O'child! You take incantation (Mantra) from us, come to our fold, become one of our disciples, get clad in special dress of Jogis or recluses, put on the blanket of beggars, hold a stick in your hand, smear ashes on your body, get your ears pierced, wear earrings of mendicants, have your head shaved clean and go from door to door playing the fiddle, or keep clapping in graveyards and cemeteries and cremation grounds; and satisfy your hunger by roaming at the pilgrimage places for food, or by asking for alms by going from house to house."

Guru Ji got a good understanding of their whole attitude from their conversation, and replied them in the form of a Shabad, Suhi Mahalla 1 Ghar 7, that is translated below:

> "Contemplation should be of Waheguru's Naam and to stay constantly in tune with Him internally. Wearing a blanket of beggars, smearing of ashes on the body, putting large earrings in your pierced ears, having the head shaved, tooting a trumpet, a cinch, or a horn, squatting in the cemeteries and wandering at the holy places do not link you with Him. These are all external showpieces. Contemplation is the name of the process that while living in the material world, we should not ensnare and entangle ourselves through misdeeds, and base actions in the mirage of the illusive materialism. We should function within materialism but it should not dictate us towards maliciousness: it should be used as a means but not allowed to become a master. We can become a real saint (Jogi) like this: Meet the Satguru, restrain the body from indulging in base actions, the mind from evil and vulgar thoughts, remember His Naam internally with such a determination and enthusiasm that our mind and soul get instrumented in the direction of Waheguru, the Creator."

There were more similar discourses with the Jogis. Finally, the Jogis yielded, conceded defeat and bowed before the Guru. They also conceded that it was his presence only that brought the fig tree back to life; they should, therefore, accord respect to him; he was a man of God. Giving up confrontational attitude, they became conciliatory and paid obeisance to Guru Ji.

Guru Ji stayed there for a few more days. People from the nearby villages became his followers (Sikhs). These adherents memorialized the spot where he sat, and had a Dharamsala, a place of worship and religion, built, and named it 'Nanak Mata'. The recognition of Jogis, thus, waned, and they all, gradually left the area.

During the life of the Sixth Guru, Sri Guru Har Gobind, Jogis returned to this place, expelled an ardent follower of the Guru, named, Almust, burnt the tree so as to erase the episode of revival of the dead tree by Guru Nanak Dev Ji. When the Sixth Guru learnt about this horrible incident, he went there, retrieved the place, gave it back to Almust, sprinkled some water on the burnt tree. We can still see the spatterings of water on the leaves of that tree. Jogis didn't remain there, but the Udasis, a sect of the followers of the Guru are the rightful owners of the nearby forest. This Gurdwara, that is near Nainital, also had a feoff endowment of five thousand rupees. First, the disciples and descendants of Almust continued to become priests here; later, a Panthic Committee, appointed by the government, started to manage its affairs. The Committee has had a beautiful temple and comfortable quarters for visitors constructed there. A fair is also held here during Diwali festival.

57. SWEET SOAP-NUT

It is also considered that Guru Ji after leaving this place went into dense forests. When Mardana got hungry, Guru Ji pointed to a fruit tree, asked him to go and eat the fruit. This was a soap-nut tree, and soap-nuts are very bitter. Mardana picked up some of them from one side, they were extremely sweet to Mardana, and were not bitter at all. The bitter fruit became sweet as soon as Guru Nanak looked and pointed towards the tree. Until now, people still bring the sweet fruits as baptismal food, and every Sikh, one time or the other, does get an opportunity to taste this blessed fruit. This tree is located about thirty miles from Nanak Mata in the forests.

58. PUNDIT CHATUR DAS

Roving around, Guru Ji came up near Benares (today known as Varanasi) at that time, also known as Kashi. A Pundit, a learned person, named Chatur Das used to live there. Finding Guru Ji on the bank of the river, the Pundit stopped and asked, "You are sitting by yourself, you don't have the small round stone nor any idol in front of you. You are not worshipping either; you do not have a rosary on your neck; you seem to be a saint; you should learn how to worship a statue and, then, become a saint."

What Guru Ji talked to him is summarized below:

> "It is not correct to do idol worship. We should worship only the Creator who is formless or shapeless. We should adore Him. At the same time, give up malicious acts; fill our minds with nectar, and the nectar is His Naam."

They kept having a long discussion. Finally, the Pundit fell at his feet and became a Sikh, a Guru's disciple. Several researchers have established that all this conversation with the Pundit that Guru Ji had, is a part of Sri Guru Granth Sahib under Ramkali Raag.

59. SRI GURU JI'S ARRIVAL IN PATNA

The city of Patna is in the state of Bihar, and is also its capital. There are ruins near it that are the tumbled down dilapidated buildings, reminders of the old town called, Patli Puttar. During the reign of emperor Chandra Gupat, Patna used to be a nine-mile long town, and around it was a wall with towers, and trenches. The wall was made up of mortar and brick. The city of Patna got inhabited again a few miles from the ruins of the old city.

During the time of Sri Guru Nanak Dev Ji, Patna was not as big as Patli Puttar used to be, but still it was a flourishing town filled with hustle and bustle. Sri Guru Ji, roving around, steering the people towards the noble acts and blessing them with new lives bringing them nearer the Lord, arrived in Patna, but did not enter the town. He encamped under the shades of beautiful trees before the town. The day was waning. It was dusk at that time. Mardana was hungry but still he performed Kirtan. Later, he started conversing with Guru Ji. The night had gone past a few hours. Mardana fell asleep but Guru Ji settled in his steady concentration, and remembrance, meditating on His Naam.

Mardana did the Kirtan, again, in the early hours. It was a rejoicing in a solitary deserted place. When it became midmorning, Mardana said, "Satguru! I slept hungry last night. I didn't have even half-full stomach of meals yesterday, either. Hunger, is again, bothering me. Our stomach is a sinner. You feed it every day and still it becomes empty every day, and beaten up by hunger, it gets increasingly irate. Let us go to town so that I can get half a pound of grains or two loaves of bread, and after eating them, I could appease my angry stomach. I do not know, on what nourishing material are you able to withstand hunger and are able to function normally under such dire circumstances?"

Then, Guru Ji, dug a shining and glittering pebble from the ground where he was sitting and giving it to Mardana, he said, "Go and sell it in town and eat whatever you like."

Mardana set out immediately and reached the town. Showing the shining stone to several shopkeepers, he, finally, arrived at the shop of Salas Rai, the jeweler. Salas, himself, was not present at the shop at that time. Two of his servants were present. One of these servants sent a word to Salas, "A vistor-stranger of a new kind is standing here, and is very anxious to sell his merchandise."

Salas Rai, and his assistant, Adhrakka, on receiving this message, both came to the shop, and started talking to the man who had already come and sat down.

"Welcome Seth Ji! Which country are you from? What merchandise have you brought with you?" [Seth: a wealthy merchant]

Who was this wealthy merchant? He was Mardana, violinist of the Guru. Hearing this, Mardana said, "I have come from mother country where five rivers flow, and I am here to sell one red shining stone. If you can give a few pennies, I would like to eat."

Salas: "Please show it."

Mardana unwrapped a small parcel and placed a shining crimson red stone weighing 5 to 6 grams before them.

Salas: (Turning it around, and looking minutely, he seemed to have been lost and then said), "Thank God. It is great! May the expert be praised. O Adhrakka! Child, bring one hundred rupees."

Adhrakka brought in one hundred rupees.

Salas: (Putting in front of Mardana) "Here is, Sir! and take your gem also; put it back into your parcel carefully."

Mardana: "Then, what are these hundred rupees for?"

Salas: (Taking a real close look at Mardana) "This 'hundred rupees' is an offering just to get a glimpse of this unusual gem. It seems that it belongs to some ace jeweler and he has sent you with it in order to put all the jewelers of the town to test, otherwise, who would like to sell this rare stone? He is fortunate who has seen such a large gem, that has such an exquisite color and is so clearly transparent, in his life time. My expert teacher often used to talk about a diamond that I have seen today with my own eyes. He used to say that if, ever, you come across a stone of such a (high) quality, you must get delighted and completely absorbed and make an offering right away. Pricewise this gem is so valuable that it is priceless. I am paying hundred rupees, which please accept as an offering (donation) for allowing me to have its glimpse."

Adhrakka: "Sir! May I also see this gem?"

Salas: (Picking up) "Here, child! See."

Adhrakka: (Looking at it again and again and was getting lost. Then he said) "Shah Ji! I have also become a connoisseur today. Truly, it is a wonderful translucent piece with absolutely true colors without any streaks. I have never before seen such brilliance, transparence, clarity and radiance as I have seen today. It continues to bring amazement."

Mardana: "Shah Ji! when my master gave this stone to me, I thought he was making fun of me. Then I said that it was a town of the sophisticated, someone will buy it for their children at least as a toy to play with, and I will be able to get enough food to fill my stomach. When I showed it to the first storekeeper, he offered me one raddish and said that his kid might be able to play with it for a little while. I demanded two and he declined. Then I went to a confectioner, he wouldn't give even two pounds of sweets; later, I stood before the store of a cloth merchant, he offered one yard of raw cotton fabric but he also advised me to take it to a goldsmith. I immediately, remembered that my master had also advised me to take it to either a goldsmith or a jeweler. Then I visited a few other shops and the value continued to rise. I became a little suspicious lest it may, truly, be an expensive piece. So looking around, I have, finally, reached you. You have put its price as priceless and offered one hundred rupees just for viewing it. I do not want to accept it."

Salas: "You take this money and the gem as well to your master. If he still chooses to sell it, please come back, but I must tell you again, it is a priceless stone."

Mardana: "Shah Ji! I am hungry since last night. My master is so contented that he does not feel the hunger. But has also not eaten. It was his command to sell it and get food."

Salas: "You please take it back. The food will also reach there. Please tell us your address and don't worry! We are merchants and your master appears to be a big merchant with an extremely keen eye. He will not be angry on this suggestion but would be pleased."

Mardana: (With his eyebrows raised) "Don't know, but he is, definitely, very big and exalted. (Then talking to himself) If he were a trader, he didn't have the necessity to roam around from place to place? He could have been fabulously rich sitting at home. (Talking in a little audible tone) O.K. I will go."

Mardana returned to Guru Ji with one hundred rupees and the gem. Satguru, seeing him, laughed, and Mardana placing the gem and the money in front of him, said, "Here is your talisman! In some places, it was not worth even two raddishes and in others, it fetched one hundred rupees just for its sight and put its value at 'priceless'."

Satguru: "Mardana! Precious items fare just like that; they become priceless in the eyes of appreciators and worthless for those with no appreciation for quality, i.e., connoisseurs consider precious things priceless and those without keen eye, consider priceless items worthless. The eyes that can recognize the intrinsic worth would place the high deserving value and those who were devoid of a sharp sense would put its value equal to a raddish. The aesthete put the value as 'limitless'. This money (one hundred rupees) is for appreciating the internal merit but we have no right to accept his money without exchanging the merchandise. Go and return the money."

Mardana was already exhausted but knew that hundred rupees didn't legitimately belong to him, and Guru Ji was not going to accept them. Therefore, whether he liked it or not, he went back to return the money.

Satguru Ji, sitting in his devotion for Waheguru in the same forest, kept humming and singing in melodiously sweet tunes:

> "O Waheguru! O Limitless; O Truthful! Our Creator! and Eliminator of our vanities! On whomsoever you become merciful, You connect him to Yourself. Meeting with You is possible only if it pleases You."

At that time Adhrakka arrived with food, cakes and other fried delicacies and was simply amazed when he heard the sweet melody; his eyes became fixed and felt some sort of strong magnetic attraction inside. He even forgot that he had come to a unique type of jeweler. He was wonderstruck within himself and started reeling with a feeling of elation. When Guru Ji finished the Shabad, placing the food before him, fell on his feet, and with folded hands, he said, "O Master! Kindly save me, protect me, I came here thinking that you will be one of the worldly jewelers but you are the embodiment of the Lord Himself. The flame inside you is spreading radiance, brilliance and splendor. O Divine Incarnation! You have blessed me with your glimpse, You put me into some sort of intoxication, You have blessed me with awareness. Kindly link me to yourself, kindly connect me, the long separated one, with yourself."

Mardana had returned by now, after dropping the money at the Salas's place. Salas got the inkling that this jeweler who did not keep the hundred rupees, didn't seem to be a worldly materialistic jeweler, rather he may be some beloved of Waheguru. He got up and followed Mardana. Having the first look at Guru Ji, he, too, became speechless. He, too, got such a flash at the first sight of Guru Ji that, being wonderstruck, he was lost in himself. Then, he pulled himself together, stepped forward and prostrated. Satguru Ji received him with courtesy and respect. With folded hands, Salas sat down and said, "I was extremely pleased to see your gem; it was amazingly rare; you are astonishingly wonderful." Keeping quiet for a moment, he asked, "Where are you from, what is your country, and what is your name?"

Satguru: "Country-Nirankar and name, Nirankari."

Salas: (Looking closely and feeling a kind of magnetism inside) "Kindly make us, too, aware of the greatness of Nirankar."

Satguru: "Waheguru who is benevolent and merciful over the poor, is omnipresesnt, I see Him pervading everywhere, He is above transmigration, He is within everyone but is still above, distinct, and separate from all."

Salas: "You can see him in all directions and everywhere, why don't we?"

Satguru: "Listen brother Salas! Both the lotus flower and the weed plant, algae, live together at the same time in clean water. Algae is unclean, but the lotus flower has some kind of sweetness, called the nectar of flowers. Both of them have the company of the same water but the lotus flower is not affected nor afflicted by the 'association blemish,' i.e. in spite of the lotus flower being so close to the algae plant, it doesn't become unclean. See again! Even the frog resides in the same water, but has no realization of the qualities of the lotus flower. He eats algae only but does not drink the sweet nectar, the ambrosial sip, from the lotus flower. The frog, constantly living in the company of lotuses, does not become aware of its virtues whereas the bees who do not live in water, coming from above, suck their qualities, the sweet ambrosial nectar from it."

Salas: "O great man! Why is it so?"

Satguru: "Lack of realization, perception, sensation, conception and cognition. The asphodels, getting a glimpse of the moon from a distance, blossom, because they have cognition. Seeing the full moon in the skies, the white lillies or asphodels who have an appreciation and realization of the moonlight also bloom."

Salas: "O God's godly person! Please explain 'realization.'"

Satguru: "Just as, your vision has full appreciation of evaluating gems and diamonds, as a jeweler, my friend and companion, Mardana, has a deep perception of musical waves, similarly, internal disposition of Nirankaris, the beloveds of Nirankar, Waheguru, is blessed with similar, in some ways and different in others, conceptual realization of Nirankar."

At this, Mardana remembered the entire first sermon given by Guru Ji; the jeweler remembered all that he had taught to his pupil, Adhrakka. The hearts were combed to clear all confusions and tangles. Salas developed love, affection, and respect in his heart. It was pretty late in the day, Salas asked them to have their meals. Satguru had refused to accept the hundred rupees saying, "the ascetics don't need it" but he ate the food, and also gave part of it (Prasad) to Mardana, which Adhrakka had served with complete devotion and dedication. Guru Ji looked at Adhrakka and blessed him.

Salas Rai: "O beloved of Nirankar! Kindly bless this servant of yours with that deep vision that can realize and see Nirankar."

Satguru Ji: "Your assistant and pupil has got that vision. He has looked closely, has been controlling himself, has seen inside himself and due to His benevolence, he has been able to see."

On this, the jeweler looked toward his assistant and fell at his feet. Satguru, looking at the liquifaction, softness and smoothness of his mind, and his sense of humility to be respectful, was greatly satisfied and pleased with Salas, so much so, that he took off his yard and a half long turban from his own head and put it on Salas's head, and throwing his vision of mercy and compassion blessed him with a lofty sight, and connected him to the Lord. This episode has been described in Suraj Prakash as follows:

> "Salas Rai tied the turban given by Guru Ji on his head. All the haziness and obscurity in his mind was cleared, He, then, had the ecstacy and elation of enlightenment and his entire inner self blossomed. With Sri Guru Nanak Sahib's kindness, compassion and mercy, a tremendous wave of love surged in him and he began to sing His praises."

This way, both Salas and his assistant, Adhrakka, were delighted and blessed and Satguru Ji uttered, "Brother! The vision of a jeweler, a musician and a poet is not easily realizable. It is unknown and beyond calculation. There is another vision that is beyond all other visions; that is what you have just been blessed with. This vision is of complete perception. When our concentration, lifting itself from the hustling and bustling world, rises in the realm of ecstasy and rapture, the self gets contained within itself, there is a flash of the infinite and the boundless, i.e., when we develop the ever present support in our minds of Him being constantly near us even though He may not be explicitly visible with our naked eyes, (but He is always there next to us), then we cross over all limits and fences. This flash leaves an indelible imprint and an everlasting impression on our minds with which we keep realizing the conception of Waheguru, Creator, the Nirankar, while operating in this live and mobile world. Now, Waheguru pervades in his memory and we may get the support and reliance of Naam at all times. Then a person, even looking at the materialistic world, does not get distracted. The visible world seems to him like a dress or appears like a room where Waheguru is visibly residing therein. Guru Ji said, "This world is a room for the truthful and the Truthful-Nirankar lives in it, and the person capable of visualizing, is willing to sacrifice himself on the intense love existing inside him."

"May I sacrifice myself on the Creator of Nature, whose infinite limits cannot be assessed."

> "O Waheguru, ever prevalent and omnipresent in the entire nature and the world! I am deeply indebted to you; and am willing to oblate and re-

> linquish myself for you. No one can assess Your boundaries, beginning or ending."

Thus, in this state of elation, full of love and affection for the Waheguru, and ecstatic in His remembrance, both Salas and Adhrakka, enjoying the blissful moments, departed. Satguru stayed there for several months. There is a spot, three miles across from the river, Ganges, where Hari Har Chhatar Fair is held every full moon. Guru Ji had stayed back for this fair so that he could pass on his message and advice among the pilgrims, take them out of the darkness of ignorance and direct them towards the light of sparklingly astute wisdom. There was, thus, a crowd around him everyday. The message was being relayed through divine Shabad Kirtan and the strayed people were moving towards the right path. This way, Sikhism was being preached and spread in the town of Patna. People would join the congregation - the holy assembly, daily, would join in the spiritual singing, and become blessed and comforted.

It was the full moon of Kartik (November), now famous for celebrating Guru Ji's birthday when he blessed the congregation of Patna, and it was on this day when he was about to leave Patna after a four-month stay there, he was asked to leave a surrogate leader for himself who should be able to steer the people in the right and noble direction. Guru Ji signalled toward Adhrakka and said, "Salas will perform the services of the leading the congregation, after whom, Adhrakka will take over."

In Patna, one of the descendants of Salas was Fateh Chand Maini, an ardent follower of the Dasam (Tenth) Guru. During his childhood, Sri Guru Gobind Singh Ji used to go to his house to play. The name of that spot came to be known as Maini Sangat.

From Adhrakka's family, two priests, Gulab Rai and Ghanshayam did serve the Tenth Guru, and many of their descendants are often seen performing service at the Patna Sahib Gurdwara. This Gurdwara was the birth place of the Tenth Guru and is called Takhat Sahib Patna Sahib, one of the five Takhats (High Seats) of the Sikhs.

Salas Rai became a devotee and a worshipper and used to write poetry as well. There are several Shabads regarding Salas in Janam Sakhis, Biographical Accounts of Saints; one of his own renderings is summarized below:

> "Satguru is the donor of Naam; He clears all haziness and opens the doors. Anyone who deals in this kind of business will never have any kind of losses. Satguru Nanak is complete, and is a heroic man of honor. He opens your eyes wide to be able to see the mysterious and

mythical spiritual secrets. The entire world is a trader and a businessman but there is only one banker - the Lord. Our business is the Satguru and our assets are His Naam. To keep singing His praises all the twenty four hours, is our humble duty. Salas prays and begs Waheguru to accede to his supplication to kindly remove our fake colorings and dye us in permanent hues."

60. GAYA

Granting salvation to Salas Rai and Adhrakka, Guru Ji left for Raj Giri. A fair was being held there where different kinds of people, who had gone astray, forgetting the path of Waheguru, had gathered. Guru Ji put them on the right track leading towards Waheguru, and making them give up malicious acts, on the way, came to Gaya. People, there, were simply amazed to see the charming, pleasing, lustrous, magnificent and radiantly brilliant face of Guru Ji, and were wondering who he was. A few Pandas (scholars) also came to the Guru. These Pandas were resident scholars at pilgrim centers. These persons would host some of the pilgrims, keep them overnight in their own homes and the pilgrims, as per their advice, would perform certain rituals for their ancestors. Under these rituals, people distributed balls of flour out of courser grains in memory of their forefathers. The Pandas asked Guru Ji to follow the same customs and get salvation for his ancestors.

Guru Ji said, "He has performed the obsequies, the last rites, and lit the lamps for himself, for his ancestors and for the entire congregation; I have performed such rites that their darkness of ignorance has been eliminated and they attained salvation when they lit a lamp of 'Naam'." That discussion was contained in a Shabad that Guru Ji recited in Raag Asa with the following central idea:

"(1) The main task for us is to meditate His Naam, i.e., to remember the Master that He is present, and present everywhere, including inside us; He is with us and loves us. We should love Him, too. With that, all our misdeeds would be condoned, and all the griefs and sorrows that follow the malicious acts will disappear.

(2) Do not be under the misconception that transgressions are not forgiven. Just as, a tiny flame can burn a huge pile of woods and reduce it to ashes, similarly, Naam will annihilate all misdemeanors.

(3) To indulge in rituals, to distribute food for the redemption of the souls of your ancestors should be rescinded in favor of meditation of the true Naam. Further, instead of roaming around the holy places like Ganges, Kashi, etc., we should devote ourselves to and love the Waheguru. That can be developed if we continue to re-

member Him constantly. This way, we will get special gratuity from Him and our lives will become worthwhile."

61. BUDH GAYA—DEV GIR

Answering questions of the Pandas and putting them on the true path, Guru Ji left Gaya. The thought that he relayed to them, and which blessed them with special eyes of knowledge and enlightenment, have already been summarized above, reading and realizing which many people had received comfort, consolation and contentment.

Leaving Gaya, Guru Sahib reached budh Gaya, about 5 miles from Gaya. Here, too, he encamped outside the town. Mardana would perform the Kirtan and then he would prevail in everlasting bliss. The Kirtan, singing of sacred hymns, attracted the attention of the priest of Budh Gaya. He came to see him. His name, as mentioned in *Khalsa History,* was Dev Gir.

This man was the priest of a Buddhist temple but was almost an ascetic. Budh Gaya was the spot in memory of Mahatma Budh. When Hindus annihilated Budhism from India, they took charge of this place as well. Sri Budh had performed penance and hard meditation and had received enlightenment here. Hindus had been opposing the Budh religion, Budhism, but had been considering Budh as an incarnation and, therefore, on that pretext, they had assumed control of this place.

Priest Dev Gir was considered very eclactic among several of the priests of smaller temples, and also well known as a great man. He was a learned person and a researcher of truth. Education and learning had made him very knowledgeable and he was a recluse, too. He had renounced the world and had no attachment with anyone and anything. But continually converting 'Raag' into renunciation and emotionalism, he had become like the branch of a tree that gets dried up after getting more and more ripened; it (the branch) became sound at the foundations but was unbendable on the top. In its steadfastness, hardness, and firmness, it had lost flexibility. This was so because there was no life left in it. A live branch retains toughness as well as maliability.

When Guru Ji explained this to Dev Gir, his understanding and intellect had a new lease. His mind became cheerful and comfortable. Guru Ji told him, "Music is love. To love misdemeanors is malicious. Therefore, have love of Waheguru alone that will ever pervade. And, we should love only good and noble actions which cleanse us and make us better persons. Again, Waheguru is an embodiment of bliss; He always remains elated, blossoming and elated, and love of Him, would take us to elation and bliss. You condemn His worldly creation and call it renunciation. This reclusion can be attained without much effort. If you love Him, you, automatically are elevated. The way you have adopted apostasy, and have killed all emotions and mental and physical feelings, any kind of love (Music) can not bend your ripened and fixed mind. It has become stiff like a ripened old branch of a tree. It is stiff like a dry piece of wood. Your mind is devoid of flexibility and firmness, and you have got the kind of stiffness that prevails in lifelessness. You have not remained as elastic as the live branch of a tree and a live mind."

This was a new lesson for Dev Gir and a new advice. His concept of reclusion was to become enlightened by killing internal sentiments, and that of contemplation, was to separate oneself by torturing one's mind. He asked Satguru, "What should I do, then? If we are not to kill organs of sense or perception, and if we are not to kill our mental desires, then what are we to do?" Satguru explained, "Brother! We have to restrain the organs of sense or perception from committing base acts, and deter our minds from indulging in low ideas. We have to give up vices and to acquire good qualities and virtues. We do not have to kill our mental love, rather to extend our mental love to connect us to Waheguru. Yes! We have to love Waheguru. We have to love Him by silently repeating His Naam, meditating His Naam, singing His praises, by praying and by being grateful to Him. The mind, this way, will be cleansed and become pure; intellect and wisdom will also become spotless and transparent. We have to steer our organs of sense and perception under the control of such a clean and an intellectual mind. We do not have to kill the love inside us. With its help and support, we have to redirect the intentions of our mind in the direction of the Lord. Once we are convinced that the source of the world is the Master, the Protector, and the Akal Purakh, the Immortal, then the only support we need and have is Waheguru Himself. When we engage the mind and intellect in acquiring deep affection for Waheguru, or by means of music, or making him our sole and solid support to develop a continuously steady attachment for Him, then Waheguru will reside within us and we will be residing within Him. Then our self will be a 'live self' and will attain the elation of salvation from transmigration. Thus, if our entire self, with all its strength will always remain engaged in 'One', then it will become contained in One, and become successful and with live knowledge. This self, this soul, is a pure spirit, and this action becomes victorious only with silently worshipping Him, or to remember the Lord and to remember Him with intense devotion. Then, we have to do it all gradually. No need of penance or hard meditation. We have to keep a deterrent on the mind by internally resolving to seek only His support, and the protection of His Naam."

After this, Guru Ji closed his eyes and the Shabad 'Harni Hovan' came out of him. Mardana understood the signal and started singing it in Gauri Bairagan through sweet tunes of his Rabab (violin):

> "If I were a doe, I would like to live in the forests where I would be picking carrots and fruits and vegetables like sweet potatoes. If with the grace of Guru, I am able to meet Waheguru, I would like to sacrifice myself again and again. I am a connoisseur of Waheguru, meaning, love Him dearly. His Naam is the merchandise. If I were a cuckoo, I would like to live in a mango tree, and give a serious gradual consideration to Naam. In the usual course, I will be able to meet with my husband, and beloved, Waheguru, whose form and glimpse projects to be so big and boundless. If I were a fish, I would like to live in water where all creatures are the epitomes of His creations. My beloved, the Waheguru, lives on both sides, I would want to meet Him with open arms. If I were a snake and live under the ground, I would still reside in the Lord's Name and Shabad within me; thus would the fears of all kinds vanish. Nanak says, as a faithful wife for ever, I will be able to reach and acquire the form of Waheguru."

Dev Gir realized in his instinct, thought and attention, and in his mind, Waheguru's Naam had settled inside. A new current started to flow inside him all the twenty four hours. He would keep his mind attached to Waheguru. Before, he was knowledgeable in his own imagination but inspite of being so scholarly, his mind used to be separated from Waheguru. During discourse, narration, discussion, consideration, thought etc., the name of the Creator or Brahma would come out of his mouth, but, now, the Waheguru was residing inside as a sweet and flavorful memory with a continuous flow. The mind that used to be scattered, weak and powerless, now remembering Waheguru, had become extremely comfortable, concentrated, and at ease.

Dev Gir kept Guru Ji with him for several days and with deep devotion, enjoyed his love for congregational gatherings and was enjoying heartily the sweetness of the Kirtan.

Guru Sahib left this place. Dev Gir, becoming extremely firm in Sikhism, continued to spread Guru Ji's message. After him, the name of the person who succeeded him in the third place was Bhagwan Gir, at which time, the Seventh Guru, Sri Guru Har Rai Ji, had succeeded on the seat of Sri Guru Nanak Dev Ji. Bhagwan came to see the Seventh Guru; enjoying the congregational meeting and having been blessed with Naam and charity, he became tranquil and contented. He, on his return, changed his dress as well, and preached Sikhism to a large number of people and converted thousands into Nanak Panthis, those who followed the path prescribed by Sri Guru Nanak Dev Ji.

62. RAJAULI

It appears that Guru Ji, after leaving Budh Gaya, came to Rajauli. Here, a Pir, named Kalhan Shah, was doing penance. He met him and seeing his self mortification and hard worship became kind and benevolent and blessed him with Naam. He, thus, made him blissful with savory Naam. Any Sikh, who meditates His Naam, considering Him to be by his side at all times, becomes an amorist, an admirer and a voluptuary and becomes a satiated connoisseur of Naam.

We hear that there are two spots in Rajauli which remind us of Guru Ji's visit there. They are called 'Bigger Congregation' and 'Smaller Congregation'.

63. KINGDOM TO A GRAZER

According to the annals, while Guru Ji was moving on, he ran into a field of grams (chick peas). In the field, was standing a young boy, its owner and caretaker, who was parching (burning) the green gram stalks. A thought occurred to Mardana that he should go to the field and eat some charred grams. Guru Ji, immediately, understood that Mardana was hungry. Therefore, with a beautiful smile, Guru Ji turned towards the field and sat down on its clean trail. The grazer-owner who was a young man, getting a glimpse of Guru Ji, was simply impressed and became filled with utmost faith and devotion. He brought some burnt grams and put them before Guru Ji, and Guru Ji, gave a handful of these cooked grams to Mardana.

At this, a thought ran through the grazer, "He is some powerful, big and eclectic saint, and happens to be hungry. I should run to my house to fetch some food for this saintly person to eat." With these thoughts, the young man got up and started to go. Guru Baba, then, asked him, "Son! Where are you going?"

He replied, "O Saintly person! I am going to bring some food from my home for you to eat. I will bring a piece of cloth as well to spread so that you may sit on it."

Guru Ji said, "This hard and bare ground of yours is like a soft quilt; your affection and faith with which you have presented the cooked (burnt) grams are like gourmet delicacies to me. Nanak is satiated with the praises of the Waheguru. You come back, do not go to your home, sit down, sit down here, you, the king." This was a casual remark but it is written in the historical books that in lieu of the burnt gram presented by the young man with utmost reverence and dedicated faith, with Guru's blessings, after a little while, he did become a real ruler of the place.

64. GOLD COINS TO CHARCOAL AND SCAFFOLD TO A PRICK

Guru Ji, then, moved on. The rainy season had set in. During these four months, the saintly people would stay in one place. They would not move around, nor go for pilgrimage.

Guru Ji had been travelling for such a long time. Bearing the intense heat, he kept going and kept blessing everyone who came in contact with him with Waheguru's Naam. Mardana was watching that the rainy season, that was considered nasty and uncomfortable, was approaching. He wished if Guru Ji would stay in one place for the duration of the rainy weather.

When Guru Ji took the fatigue of travel on himself, Mardana would be bashful not to relay his own tiredness, hunger and any other needs so as not to burden the Guru with his problems, but would rather be explicit to others to convey his needs and wants so that he could receive the attention and hospitality wherever feasible. Guru Ji had been travelling since the past spring and had not stayed for long any where; at the most for a few days at one place, spreading the preachings of the Waheguru's Naam and would, then move on. Now the rains had set in. Mardana wanted very much that his charming and beautiful master, Guru Ji, should take rest for a few days. He, therefore, suggested, "Guru Ji! Could we spend these rainy days in some abode. The weather has turned offensive and nasty." Guru Ji, respecting and appreciating his affection, said, "As soon as we hit a town, we will spend the rainy season there."

So moving along, with Waheguru's kindness and benevolence, they reached a high dry plateau, a pleasant place, near a nice town. This was about a mile outside the town. Guru Ji decided to encamp there. Mardana was pleased that the perennial unending travels were over, even though only for the rainy season. My beloved master, at least for some days, would go to sleep and eat his meals on time, and would be little comfortable.

There was a substantial population in that village like a small town. A well-to-do Khatri used to live there, who had an attachment and inclination towards the spiritual and religious way of life. He would see any visiting saint to town and would do his bit to try to make him comfortable and welcomed. He would perform service and worship as well. He heard, "On the outskirts of the town, some saintly person has encamped in one deserted room, who appeared extremely loving and pleasant. The Kirtan performed there daily is so awe inspiring, melodious and fulfilling that even flowing rivers stop their current to listen." This man came to see Guru Ji. Sri Guru Ji was sitting collected and conjoined with Waheguru in his own lovable divine mood. A cool breeze was blowing and Mardana was performing Kirtan with great devotion and love. The Khatri bowed before Guru Ji and sat down. Immediately thereafter, his eyes closed down and he became engrossed in the savory and delight of the atmosphere. He didn't keep track of where the time went by. When the Khatri opened his eyes, he realized that much time had elapsed. Khatri appreciated that this Kirtan was truly a chaste, divine rendering, that can win over even the death. He had never heard such a Kirtan before, that would make the passing of a substantial amount of time completely unfelt, such a Kirtan that he completely lost himself into. Then, he would look at Guru Ji and kept saying, "I have never seen such a saintly face before." His mind was so bewitched that he was dancing in elation like a peacock, around the Guru, didn't want to go away at all. How charming Guru Ji looked?

This way, the Khatri was enchanted. When he remembered his business and other chores and the pull of some of the worldly activities, he returned home, after some time. He kept coming back again and again and would enjoy the delight of the divine Kirtan. In the Khatri's mind, the attraction for the Guru kept building day by day. The attraction increased so much that he pledged that he would continue to come everyday to have an eclectic glimpse of the Guru. If he were unable to come on anyday, he would not eat or drink anything that day. Thus, he made it a daily routine to come, to have godly sight of Guru Ji and to listen to the spiritual Kirtan.

One day, another shopkeeper, an acquaintance of the Khatri, asked him, "Where do you go everyday?" He replied, "Brother! A complete person, a true saint has encamped outside the town. I go to see him." The shopkeeper asked him to take him along, too, on his next trip there. The Khatri readily agreed and said, "Sure! Please come along, and have his divine glimpse."

Next time, the shopkeeper tagged along, but after a little way, the shopkeeper took up a different route and reached an area where evil people had assembled. There he got involved in wicked actions and seemed to be enjoying himself.

Both of them started to come together everyday but up to a certain point. Therefrom, the Khatri would go to the saintly congregation of Guru Ji, and the shopkeeper to the evil company of base people. Khatri would try to explain to him not to go to ungodly and sinful people's company but go with him to the company of noble and chaste persons. The shopkeeper, however, would not listen. One day, the shopkeeper suggested, "Well! Whosoever reaches here first today, should wait at the junction of these routes under the fig tree. We will go home together."

On that day, the shopkeeper returned rather early and sat down at the appointed spot to wait for his friend, Khatri. Sitting idle, he started scratching the ground. When he removed some dirt from the surface, he found a gold coin buried there. The shopkeeper was delighted; he took it out and tied it to his waist; took out his knife and started scratching and digging more. While digging deeper and deeper, he found a pot buried there. When he looked inside, he found only charcoal in the entire pot.

In the meantime, the Khatri also arrived there. The shopkeeper saw that he had a bandage on his foot and he was limping. He was wearing only one shoe but had tied his other shoe with a broken sole to the other foot. He asked the Khatri, "What happened to your foot?" The Khatri replied, "A thorn got stuck in." The shopkeeper, then, taunted him, "You everyday pushed me towards going to the holy assembly. See what has happened to you for going to the spiritual congregation. On the other hand, even though I have been involved with bad company engaged in wicked acts, I found a gold mohar. You have been dissuading me from evil company and evil action. Let us go and ask your saintly person, how is it that good actions ended up in a thorn piercing in you, and my base actions resulted in finding a gold mohar?"

Both of them came to Guru Ji; touched his feet and started asking the question. Guru Ji told them, "O you shopkeeper! The pot of charcoal was full of gold mohars. You might have given one gold mohar to some beloved of Waheguru sometime. You were about to receive a reward one thousand times of your donation. But as you got more and more involved in malicious actions and kept committing more and more sins, the fruits of your earlier good actions kept falling down i.e., your sins burnt up all the fruits collected for your good actions. You are left with only one noble act that had brought you here. You should understand that this one mohar is relaying you the message that your sinful acts have removed many like it from your luck; instead of turning into green all that you had sown, the bad company has scorched everything, and changed into charcoal. Your Khatri friend has been coming to the holy assembly, been listening to the singing of holy hymns, has heard and remembered Naam, has performed service to the saintly persons, and has, thus, been able to wipe off all his sins. He had done some bad acts earlier, the results of which would have been to hang him. As he continued to attend and perform service in the holy congregation, continued to develop love for Waheguru, and continued to remember Him by repeating silently His Naam, his sins and bad luck were getting annihilated and dissipated until the extreme pain of scaffolding was reduced to just that of a thorn prick, and saved him from the extreme misery of death. Think again, brother! Bad actions kept on corrupting you more and more: your desire for evil acts continued to increase. On the other hand, as your friend, the Khatri, continued to participate in congregational assemblies, his mind got more and more purified. His thoughts were directed more and more towards noble acts, public service, and his love for Waheguru. His mind became clean and an admirer of good living."

Hearing this advice, the shopkeeper felt a jolt inside. His mind accepted that whatever Guru Ji was saying was correct and appropriate. He trembled; the touch of Guru's hand was like a hot fire, with which all his sins were burnt. He fell on his feet and said, "Kindly take mercy on me; put me on the right path; teach me only good actions and prevent me from evil deeds. Kindly include me, the sinner, too, in the company of saintly persons."

Guru Ji sermonized him on the Naam of Waheguru, and his entire disposition was completely changed. He became a person who would do noble acts, give charities, practice religion and became a lover and a connoisseur of Waheguru. His entire life became worthwhile and successful.

Guru Ji made the following pronouncement at that time:

(Maru Mahalla 1 Ghar 1)

"According to our actions, good or bad, we keep writing our destinies. The human beings, therefore, steer their lives as per these actions. What performs actions is our body. The body is like a piece of paper, and the mind is the inkpot, and whatever people do, good or bad, are written down as their inclinations or their characters. O people with insane minds! remember the Waheguru. If you become afraid of Him, you will engage in noble acts. Think! You lose virtues and add to your vices if you keep on forgetting Him.

O folks! You spend the night in carelessness and ignorance and the day in conducting your business in useless, worthless and evil activities, i.e., you get yourself engaged every hours of day and night in actions that just entrap you, just as a bird gets ensnared in a cage under the greed of receiving the bird feed. A net was spread already under the feed. Similarly, you, every moment, under some pretext (greed) or the other, in pursuit of the pleasure of flavory tastes, keep falling down from your religious principles. Doing wicked deeds, we acquire an evil character, and get entrapped in it.

Tell me O people! How would you get riddance from such a noose? Your body is hot like an oven; your mind is the iron inside it; five fires of greed, lust, anger, attachment and pride are burning there; more and more charcoal (of sins) are being added to the fire; the mind is burning in them; apprehension is performing the functions of a pair of pliers, i.e., apprehension is turning the iron (mind) over and over again, due to which the heat of the fire continues to burn us constantly. This way, the mind being burnt again and again becomes a slag or a dross of iron (almost like a dirt). But do not despair, my friends! once the mind becomes slag, it can become not only iron but gold also."

Question: "What is the technique to convert slag into gold?"
Answer: "You have to have a special Guru (teacher)."
Question: "What kind?"
Answer: "Someone who has the knowledge and experience of changing dross into gold. That is a touchstone, a metal when touched immediately converts any metal into gold. Therefore, a Guru like a touchstone, can convert human beings into gods and angels.

That Guru should bless you with the only Naam. What kind of Naam? Nectar Naam, sweet like nectar, and the one able to revive the dead into live beings. Meditating His Naam, your body and mind will become settled with chastity, and purity.

65. EMANCIPATION OF THUGS

From there, Guru Ji moved on. On the way, he met a bunch of thugs (cheats, swindlers, tricksters or robbers). Guru Ji had the radiance of Naam on his face; the brow was cheerful, and brilliant. The swindlers assumed that he must be a wealthy person, all this radiance is that of money; they all surrounded him. When they looked at him closely, they became somewhat inert and dilatory. Guru Ji asked them, "Who are you, people?" One of them spontaneously said, "We are thugs, and have come to kill you." Guru Ji, then, in a forceful voice, without any fear, said, "May God bless you. Please do kill me if you so desire, but please do perform one chore for me first." They asked, "What is that?"

Guru Ji said, "Go and bring some fire from that distant smoke, and after killing me, place my body on this pile of wood and ignite the fire."

Two of the thugs said, "We have killed so many persons, but no one had ever conceded laughingly to be killed, and the excuse that he is employing to delay his execution will not work. Where can he go escaping from us?"

Two of the thugs ran to fetch fire. It was a burning pyre. They saw a few faces before the pyre whom people call angels or gods. They are not, usually, visible, but they became manifest to these thugs. These thugs asked them, "Who are you and what are you doing?" One of them said, "This person, whose pyre is burning, was a great sinner. He was going to go to most torturing and dreadful hell. The godly Guru whom you have surrounded to kill, put one look at his pyre. With his sacred glance, all sins of this man have been burnt. Now, we are here to take him to the heavens."

Those thugs started shivering in terror and started thinking, "What a great man should he be whom we are about to kill." They came running and fell at Guru Ji's feet.

The rest of the gang were surprised and asked them, "What has happened, fellows?" Then, these two thugs narrated the entire episode that they had seen and experienced. Hearing that, all of them shuddered in their trousers. With folded hands, all of them prayed, "O Great and noble soul! We are great sinners, we have committed numerous transgressions. Kindly erase our sins and bless us."

Guru Ji said, "Give up all these transgressive acts; whatever wealth you have swindled, cheated or robbed from the people, distribute it away to the poor, the needy, and to the saintly people. Engage yourself in some honest farming activities etc., then only your sins will be forgiven."

They all agreed to accept Guru Ji's advice and command. Guru Ji blessed them with benevolent Naam, put them into an honest line of work, and linked them to virtuous deeds instead of sinful actions. Satguru Ji, at that time, recited a Shabad that is summarized below (Sri Raag Mahalla 1):

> "The Guru recounted malicious acts in this hymn. He has called greed a dog, telling a lie, a scavenger, swindling as eating of dead body, vituperation of others putting filth in your own mouth and anger as the

wretched untouchable that can burn us like fire. He also said that the entire world is absorbed in these malicious acts, self praise and other similar savors.

Gold, silver, beauty, fragrances, horses, elaborate beds, palaces, buildings, meats and sweets, all these are considered physical pleasures. If we are preoccupied with so many pleasures, how can Naam reside in that heart? It can't.

He also said that to talk coarsely and insipidly is humiliation in itself. We should talk only something that is pleasant and acceptable, and which can grant us a place and respect in the land of Waheguru. Blessed are those who are loved by the Benefactor. Doing good deeds in His land are considered noble acts. Evil actors will be left out in the cold crying.

They have chaste intellect and are honorable in whose hearts does Waheguru reside, and they have in their possession the true wealth. They cannot be praised enough. Nobody can be good but them, because persons devoid of blessing cannot get involved in Naam and virtuous deeds."

As Guru Ji travelling to different places, was putting good people on the noble path, blessing them with the sermon of Naam, and granting them emancipation, similarly, going to evil people, he was instrumental in deterring them from committing evil acts and directing them towards honest line of work. He would, thus, convert those who were tormenting, troubling and torturing the world into pleasurable and comforting individuals. He would arouse love for Waheguru, virtue and kindness in them and would bless them with redemption from transmigration.

"Dhan Sri Guru Nanak Dev Ji
Great was, is and will be
Sri Guru Nanak Dev Ji Nirankari."

September 8, 1988

AN APPEAL FOR FUNDS

THE SIKH YOUTH FORUM

(Non-Profit Tax-Exempt Organization)

OBJECTIVES:

1. To engage in religious, cultural, educational and social activities including youth camps, Sunday and other types of schools, seminars, conferences and discussion groups;
2. To promote and disseminate religious, educational, social and cultural aspects of Sikh religion and other religions/groups from the Indian sub-continent;
3. To establish and maintain Sikh Youth Centers and other similar Centers in different parts of the United States;
4. To hold congregations for specific and general purposes for understanding the tenets of Sikhism and other religions on a regular and ad hoc basis;
5. To publish a periodical/magazine/newsletter; and
6. To interface its activities with other organizations/institutions with similar objectives.

During the past 11 years, the Sikh Youth Forum, Washington, DC independently and in collaboration with those interested in Sikh religious educational development, has organized 22 Sikh youth camps with durations from 3 to 12 days. It is gratifying that a little over 850 Sikh children of ages 6–22 have gone through them. These children came from across America; from the states of Virginia, Maryland, New York, New Jersey, Pennsylvania, Illinois, Ohio, Florida, Georgia, Louisiana, Connecticut, Alabama and California. The curricular activities during these Camps included instruction in Sikh History, Shabad Kirtan, Gurmukhi, Punjabi speaking, Nit Nem, Sikh Values, and discussions/information on current Sikh issues, and social issues in the western society. Special efforts are directed towards the public speaking aspect of an individual's development. Children in groups would prepare reports on assigned topics and were asked to present their reports to the general public on the concluding day. New and continuing children, and children of broadly different age groups, were given separate instructions at their appropriate levels.

One can have an humble sense of achievement in raising the consciousness of the population about Sikh religious education to be started at an early age in an alien environment but, certainly, it should not be a source of any kind of complacency. A little has been done and a lot more still needs to be tackled for which financial contributions/ donations are solicited.

The Sikh Youth Forum
P.O. Box 7061
Gaithersburg, MD 20898

AN APPEAL FOR FUNDS

THE WASHINGTON SIKH CENTER

(Non-Profit Tax-Exempt Organization)

OBJECTIVES:

1. To promote the values of Sikhism and religious interests of Sikhs;
2. To enhance the image of Sikhs and to promote their status and their rights in the religious, social, cultural, educational, economic and political fabric of the society;
3. To educate the members of the Sikh community, particularly the children, about the Sikh religious teachings as embodied in Sri Guru Granth Sahib and to promote Sikh practices through regular services (including Shabad Kirtan, Shabad Katha, teaching of Gurmukhi, etc.), and other appropriate activities;
4. To disseminate "information" about the religious, social, cultural, and educational aspects of Sikhs and Sikhism; and
5. To promote unity among Sikhs and to cooperate with other organizations (a) in the achievement of the above objectives, and (b) for the welfare of the disadvantaged segments of the society.

The Washington Sikh Center is presently engaged in building a Gurdwara in Gaithersburg, MD in suburban Washington, DC. A 1.6 acre tract of land in the heart of the commercial district has already been acquired. We desperately need financial contributions/ donations for the building to be erected. The plans have been finalized and are going through the county scrutiny. All moneys are tax deductible. A donation of $5,000 would entitle the donor to be a patron and a life member of The WSC and will be of immense benefit to this organization.

The Washington Sikh Center
P.O. Box 7061
Gaithersburg, MD 20898

TRANSLATOR

Ujagar Singh Bawa is presently Professor of Economics and formerly Associate Vice President for Academic Affairs at Bloomsburg University of Pennsylvania. He has also taught at Wilkes College and Howard University. He has worked as Manager, Econometric Research and the Chief Economist and later as a Consultant to Data Transmission Company, Vienna, VA. He was formerly a Senior Research Officer and Head, Inter Industry Study Group, Planning Commission, a member of the Central Economic Service and held positions of responsibility with the Government of India in the Press Commission, Ministry of Agriculture, and the Cabinet Secretariat.

Dr. Bawa received his B.A. and M.A. degrees in mathematics from the Punjab University. He then specialized in mathematical statistics at the Institute of Agricultural Research Statistics, New Delhi where he obtained a Post Graduate Certificate and a Diploma (one year each), recognized equivalent to a Master's degree, in statistics. He received his Master's degree in economics from the Wharton School of University of Pennsylvania and his Ph.D. from Cornell University.

Professor Bawa has written numerous research papers in economics and statistics, some of which he has presented to national and international conferences and/or had published in prestigious professional journals. He is author of several research papers on Sikhism, Sikh education and Sikh issues. Some of them are: The Analysis of Recent Sikh Tragedy; The Sikh Case; Fairness for Sikhs; Information Propaganda and Draconian Laws, Censorship and Misrepresentations; Keshadhari, Sehajdhari and Non Keshadhari; Saint-Soldier Concept and the Sikh Gurus; Religious Education and the Sikh Youth Abroad; Sikhism and the Identity Crisis; Sacrifice; An Essay on a Glimpse of Sikh History; Meditation and Naam; Sri Guru Tegh Bahadur Ji; Gurmat Naam; Meditation and Naam; The Sikh Tenets, A Short Essay on Sikhism; The Sikhs and the Indian Presidency; Treatment of Minorities under a Majority Rule; Political Remedy and the Oppression of Sikhs; and The Punjab Dilema.

In addition, Dr. Bawa has authored and published a monograph on *Sikhism*. Dr. Bawa has translated other classic works of Bhai Sahib Dr. Vir Singh from Punjabi to English: (1) *Satwant Kaur*
(2) Balam Sakhian Dasam Guru

Published in 1989 by
The Washington Sikh Center
The Sikh Youth Forum
P.O. Box 7061
Gaithersburg, MD 20898

ISBN: 0-942245-04-0 (Paper back)